Revised Edition

The Great Outdoors

Advocating for Natural Spaces for Young Chidren

Mary S. Rivkin With Deborah Schein

National Association for the Education of Young Children
Washington, DC

National Association for the Education of Young Children
1313 L Street NW, Suite 500
Washington, DC 20005-4101
202-232-8777 • 800-424-2460
www.naeyc.org

NAEYC Books

Chief Publishing Officer
Derry Koralek

Editor-in-Chief
Kathy Charner

Director of Creative Services
Edwin C. Malstrom

Managing Editor
Mary Jaffe

Senior Editor
Holly Bohart

Senior Graphic Designer
Malini Dominey

Associate Editor
Elizabeth Wegner

Editorial Assistant
Ryan Smith

Through its publications program, the National Association for the Education of Young Children (NAEYC) provides a forum for discussion of major issues and ideas in the early childhood field, with the hope of provoking thought and promoting professional growth. The views expressed or implied in this book are not necessarily those of the Association or its members.

Permissions

The table "The Relationship Between Nature and Human Health," on page 9, is adapted with permission from F.E. (Ming) Kuo, "Parks and Other Green Environments: Essential Components of a Healthy Human Habitat," Executive Summary (Ashburn, VA: National Recreation and Park Association, 2010), 2. www.nrpa.org/uploadedFiles/nrpa.org/Publications_and_Research/Research/Papers/MingKuo-Summary.PDF.

The box "No One Has Fun When They Are Cold: Clothes for the Outdoors," on page 24, is reprinted by permission from C. Lambert, The DragonFly (Dodge Nature Preschool newsletter, Fall/Winter 2010): 7. www.dodgenaturecenter.org.

The box "Don't Fear the Reaper," on page 82, is reprinted by permission from K. Finch, "Design Principles for Nature Play Spaces in Nature Centers and Other Natural Areas," (Omaha, NE: Green Hearts Institute for Nature in Childhood, 2009), 3. www.greenheartsinc.org/uploads/Green_Hearts_Design_Principles_for_Nature_Play_Spaces.pdf.

Credits

Cover design: Edwin Malstrom

Photographs

Cover photograph: © Jude Keith Rose

Courtesy of the authors: 60, 67, 85, 88, 92; Barbara Bent/© NAEYC: 5; © Bonnie Blagojevic: 68; Bonnie Blagojevic/© University of Maine Center for Community Inclusion and Disability Studies: 6; Courtesy of Mark Brennan: 23; Peg Callaghan/© NAEYC: 15, 62; © Frances Carlson: 75, 83; © Walter Drew: 94; © Stephanie Frey/Thinkstock: vii; Courtesy of Mary Hardcastle: 73; Courtesy of Rebecca Harper: 70; Higher Horizons/© NAEYC: 40; © Elisabeth Nichols: ix, 39; © Karen Phillips: 16, 19, 25, 31, 33, 37, 43, 49; © Ellen Senisi: 8, 17, 41, 45, 51, 57, 63; Susan Woog Wagner/© NAEYC: 1, 81, 95; Used with permission from www.pedbikeimages.org/Chris Metka: 91

Library of Congress Control Number: 2013951457

ISBN: 978-1-928896-99-9

Item 178

Contents

Foreword

> A degraded habitat will produce degraded humans. If there is to be any true
> progress, then the entire life community must progress.
>
> —Thomas Berry

I n the 1990s, when Mary Rivkin first set out to advocate for outdoor play, only a handful of researchers and academic thinkers in the United States were giving this issue the attention it deserved. Her 1995 book *The Great Outdoors: Restoring Children's Right to Play Outside* made an early and convincing case that children should have the right to experience the natural world through the most natural of ways: play.

Poets, literary giants, conservationists, and designers—such as John Muir, Frederick Law Olmsted, Rachel Carson, Aldo Leopold, E.O. Wilson, and ecotheologian Thomas Berry—had already given shape to this driving idea: Human beings have an inborn affiliation with the rest of the natural world, and our hunger for and love of nature is essential to our humanity. In the 1970s, Robin Moore and Joseph Cornell applied this principle to where children play. Others, including authors Louise Chawla, Robert Michael Pyle, and David Sobel, deepened the conversation. Environmental educators, including Judy Braus, Jon Young, and Cheryl Charles, added to the gathering wisdom and applied it. The list of early heroes goes on.

Since then, the academic world has awakened from its slumber. A growing number of studies point to the deficit of nature experience among children and to the benefits of such experience.

Because this fragile awakening is relatively new, most of the evidence is correlative, not causal—but this burgeoning body of research points in one direction: Experiences in the natural world offer tangible psychological and physical benefits, help children learn, and build conservation values. Time in nature can, for some children, reduce the symptoms of attention deficit/hyperactivity disorder, calming them and helping them focus. Natural play spaces and nature learning areas in schools can help children improve academically and play more creatively. Nature experience can be a buffer to obesity and overweight. In cities, biodiversity can have a profound impact on the mental health of children and adults and can build social capital.

Yes, we need more research, but according to Howard Frumkin, dean of the University of Washington School of Public Health, "we know enough to act." Echoing the nature study movement of the early part of the twentieth century, a new nature movement has emerged. Changing hearts, minds, and legal codes, this movement is stimulating new ways to design schools, neighborhoods, and cities; providing new tools for conservation and sustainability; inspiring action among pediatricians and other health professionals; and giving parents and teachers a powerful agent to balance children's lives and their own.

Now, in this revised edition of *The Great Outdoors,* Mary Rivkin offers one of the clearest, most practical, most concise, and usable guides to moving the movement. We need this book, and others like it to come.

Progress is now visible, but the barriers between human beings and nature remain, and some are growing. Among them are the ongoing destruction of healthful habitats for humans and animals; poor design of cities, neighborhoods, homes, schools, and workplaces; media-amplified fear of strangers; real dangers in some neighborhoods, including traffic and toxins; the "criminalization" of natural play through social attitudes, city ordinances, and community covenants; a litigious society that favors risk-free environments that, ironically, can lead to greater risks later; and the dominance of digital technology in almost every aspect of our lives. Technology is not, in itself, the enemy, but our society's lack of balance is lethal. The pandemic of inactivity is one result. Sitting is the new smoking.

In these refreshed pages of *The Great Outdoors,* Mary Rivkin applies her keen intellect and generous heart to the ultimate goal: deep, self-replicating cultural change. Every child—not just the ones whose parents appreciate nature, not only those of a certain economic class or culture or set of abilities—*every* child has a human right to the gifts of nature and play.

—Richard Louv, author of *Last Child in the Woods* and *The Nature Principle,* and chairman emeritus of the Children and Nature Network

Introduction

When I was doing research for the first edition of *The Great Outdoors*, which was published in 1995, information about children and the outdoors was sparse. What I found included Roger Hart's (1978) study of children's outdoor experiences in a small Vermont town—where they liked to play, how much parental supervision they had, how they interacted with the physical environment—and Robin Moore's (1986) study of children navigating their communities in southwest England. The journal *Children's Environments Quarterly* presented many smaller studies, some of which were about the outdoors.

Joe Frost had produced a body of playground research, much of it concerned with safety and design. It was he who stimulated my interest in the topic of children's outdoors experiences by asking me to write a chapter on the benefits of outdoor play in 1986. I quickly discovered the lack of research on this subject—we all simply *believed* that outdoor play was good for children.

In addition, outdoor play opportunities for children were vanishing. That problem was the focus of the first edition of *The Great Outdoors*. The problem still bedevils us, but now, nearly 20 years later, the research is flourishing. It includes the work of Frances Ming Kuo and many others who document how nature experiences benefit everyone, especially children. Also of note is the study of children in cities headed by Louise Chawla (2002) and the work of Richard Louv, who established the Children and Nature Network and wrote the groundbreaking and thought-provoking books *Last Child in the Woods: Saving Our Children From Nature-Deficit Disorder* (2005; 2008) and *The Nature Principle: Reconnecting With Life in a Virtual Age* (2012).

About This Book

In this revised edition of *The Great Outdoors,* I hope to do justice to all the excellent research and advocacy work that supports children's outdoor play and learning. Although this book mainly concerns trends and experiences in the United States, I occasionally note what is happening in other countries as an example of what we in the United States could do to bolster children's involvement with the natural world.

Chapter 1, "Children and the Outdoors," reviews why outdoor play matters for children, provides a summary of the research on its benefits—especially when it involves nature—outlines barriers to outside play, and describes important efforts to increase children's time in the outdoors.

Chapter 2, "Early Childhood Settings With Outdoors in Mind," explores the historical and contemporary inspirations and foundations for nature education and outdoor exploration.

Chapter 3, "Precautions Outdoors," discusses ways to keep children safe outdoors, including minimizing sun exposure and other dangers.

Chapter 4, "Children's Spiritual Development and Nature," highlights the importance of nature experiences for children's spiritual development, an overlooked topic in the early childhood literature.

Chapter 5, "Cities for Children," explores the necessity and challenges of creating child-friendly cities and environments.

My hope is that the information and views presented in this book will inspire more educators to advocate for children to spend time outdoors, have safe outdoor environments, and be free to learn through outdoor exploration.

1

Children and the Outdoors

D o you feel relaxed when spending time outdoors in a quiet place? If so, perhaps you will relate to what Christie, a mother and teacher, writes about walking in the woods.

While walking in the woods, I feel less stressed. The coolness of the shaded trees, the sight of wildlife, and the smell of the woods—it's the smell of my childhood. It makes me happy.

There are so many things in the woods that make me feel like a young girl again. When I walk over the small bridge that crosses a stream, I have an overwhelming urge to climb down to the water's bank, take off my shoes, and feel the cold water on my toes. The trails, some well-defined and others thick with trees, spark my curiosity. I wonder where they lead. I recall times in my youth when I drifted into the woods . . . yet was never really scared when I found myself on an unfamiliar trail. To me, wandering in the woods is liberating. It is freedom.

As I walk, I notice many beautiful sights. I see a group of three deer roaming in the woods. Once the deer notice me, they gracefully hop away. Next, I notice a patch of wild mushrooms, no doubt a result of all of the recent rainfall. The mushrooms differ in size and shape and are literally everywhere. I bend down to touch one—cold and soft. Deeper in the woods I find a beautiful chrysalis hanging from a low branch. When I look around, I recognize the oak and beech trees. The leaves are changing and have lovely shades of color.

The woods have a profound effect on me. Being a single mom of three and a full-time graduate student, I've been running on fumes for the past few years. A walk in a natural area always has a calming effect on me: My breathing slows, my senses tingle, and I actually feel lighter. This "green time" is so important to my wholeness as a person, but I sometimes ignore my longing for it. Although I have a busy schedule, this short time spent in the woodland helped me realize I desperately *need* to reprioritize my schedule. Even a mere thirty minutes a week of green time is beneficial to my heart and soul!

—Christie Cioffi

In the first edition of *The Great Outdoors* I wrote, "Children's access to outdoor play has evaporated like water in sunshine. It has happened so fast, along with everything else in this speed-ridden century, that we have not coped with it." Since the publication of that book in 1995, awareness of and concern about children's vanishing opportunities for outdoor play have only increased among adults who understand the importance of such play to children's development.

Article 29 of the Convention on the Rights of the Child states that education should foster "the development of respect for the natural environment" (UN General Assembly 1989, 9).

The subtitle of the first edition was *Restoring Children's Right to Play Outside*. The concept of children's rights stems from decades-old work that culminated in the United Nations Convention on the Rights of the Child in 1989. Article 31 of this document states that among children's overall rights to survival, development, protection, and participation is the right to leisure and play (UN General Assembly 1989).

Several states in the United States have adapted this concept and issued proclamations on children's right to play outdoors (see, for example, Maryland's proclamation in the sidebar). Although the right to play outside is not yet a *legal* right in the United States, it has long been a broadly supported *cultural* right. One of the founders of the modern environmental movement, Aldo Leopold, declared that for some of us, "the chance to find a pasque-flower is a right as inalienable as free speech" (1949, xvii). Richard Louv, author of *Last Child in the Woods: Saving Our Children From Nature-Deficit Disorder* (2005; 2008), has done a great deal to persuade the general public

Proclamation
Maryland Children's Outdoor Bill of Rights

WHEREAS, Children across the globe are losing their connection with our natural world, an alienation that threatens their health, their quality of life, their readiness for future job opportunities and the future of our natural resources;

WHEREAS, Children who spend frequent time outdoors enjoying unstructured and structured activity experience enhanced use of the senses, fewer attention difficulties and decreased rates of physical and emotional illness and obesity;

WHEREAS, Spending frequent time outdoors is also the best way to develop a connection to nature and the foundation on which to build an environmental stewardship ethic;

WHEREAS, The State of Maryland is committed to ensuring all children have the opportunity to connect with nature at an early age and build upon that connection throughout their developing years;

NOW, THEREFORE,

I MARTIN O'MALLEY GOVERNOR OF THE STATE OF MARYLAND BY VIRTUE OF THE AUTHORITY VESTED IN ME BY THE CONSTITUTION AND THE LAWS OF MARYLAND, HEREBY PROCLAIM THAT EVERY MARYLAND CHILD SHALL HAVE THE OPPORTUNITY TO . . .

- Discover and connect with their natural world.
- Play and learn outdoors.
- Splash and swim in the water.
- Camp under the stars.
- Follow a trail.
- Catch a fish.
- Watch wildlife.
- Explore wild places close to home.
- Celebrate their culture and heritage.
- Share nature with a great mentor or teacher.

From State of Maryland, "Maryland Children's Outdoor Bill of Rights," 2009. www.governor.maryland.gov/documents/OutdoorBillOfRights.pdf.

to support children's access to outdoor play and experiences. He notes that with new research supporting the value of nature experiences for children and demonstrating that the lack of such experiences is detrimental to children's development, the right to outdoor play is analogous to a civil right. As Louv notes in *The Nature Principle: Reconnecting With Life in A Virtual Age*, "As a society, we need to give nature back to our children and ourselves. To not do so is immoral. It is unethical" (2012, 268).

The subtitle of this new edition, *Advocating for Natural Spaces for Young Children,* reflects a major challenge for those of us concerned about children and the outdoors: providing an abundance of safe, clean, and interesting places for children to play and explore the natural world. This chapter will

- Discuss why outdoor play matters for children
- Summarize the research on the benefits of outdoor play and involvement with nature
- Outline barriers to outdoor play
- Describe efforts by national and regional organizations to increase children's time in the outdoors

Like the first edition, this book focuses on children in preschool, kindergarten, and the early primary grades.

Reasons for Outdoor Play

Sana, who is 4, enjoys exploring the outdoor play area behind her preschool. One bright spring day, she gathers a bouquet of dandelions. Seeing her teacher, she holds up the flowers and says, "I picked these for you."

In his tree-filled yard Keown, 5, invents a variety of activities. He uses his shovel to dig holes, many holes. He digs silently and alone, his sweaty face revealing his concentration. Keown also enjoys gathering sticks and piling them in the yard. He adds sticks he has gathered during neighborhood walks and weekend hikes with his family. One day his mother counts the collection—80 sticks, all different, all precious.

Young children have always used the outdoors for exploring, creating, inventing. We observe them in their play and wonder, what are they thinking and feeling? What will they remember from these times? Do they have enough opportunities to interact with natural materials and with other people outside? Will their outdoor experiences support their development and give them enjoyment now and in the future?

New delights and opportunities for learning await children each time they venture outdoors. There are many reasons for outdoor play; here are some I believe are the most important.

Humans *Are* Nature

The sociobiologist Edward O. Wilson (2008) hypothesizes that humans are innately drawn to other living things, that *biophilia,* "love of nature/living organisms," is our evolutionary inheritance. Not only does nature supply our material needs, it gives us "aesthetic, intellectual, cognitive, and even spiritual meaning and satisfaction" (Kellert & Wilson 1993, 20). If we consider Wilson's biophilia hypothesis in the light of the confinements of modern schools, homes, and vehicles, and reflect on how relatively new in history these environments are, our way of life seems a stark departure from the past. To be fully human we need to connect with nature.

The theologian philosopher Thomas Berry develops the concept further—we *are* nature. We have not evolved beyond nature, we are still inextricably linked, and as a species we must consciously re-engage with the world so that our co-evolution becomes positive and protective, not destructive (Berry 1999).

Children Are Multisensory, Physical Beings

Children are growing, moving organisms who need time during and after the school day to expend energy, explore the world outdoors, and develop a variety of skills. As Yi Fu Tuan (1993) says,

> The education of a child is a constant reminder that the child is nature, that its body is nature. . . . Pure and simple happiness, intense pleasure, and the regeneration of life all depend on the natural functions of a healthy body. (228)

In early childhood settings, children need time to explore literacy, math, science, and more through both indoor and outdoor activities. This approach ensures young children's healthy development and learning. And nature, according to contemporary physics, is matter and energy in continual motion—a perfect description of a typical young child. We are born to move and to learn from moving.

Outdoor Play Is Liberating

Being outdoors provides a sense of freedom that is different from the freedom children experience during indoor play. This is significant for both

teachers and children. Not only is there usually more space out of doors, there are fewer objects in that space to bump into, break, or lose parts of. Outdoors, children can shout, sing, jump, roll, and stretch without the confines of walls and ceilings. Outdoor voices are acceptable. Children are more carefree.

When the outdoor play area is physically safe—free from hazards and dangerous equipment—teachers can engage with children in play and exploration rather than having to focus on setting and enforcing safety rules. Children can decide what to do and who to play with. In a well-designed outdoor play area, children can safely experiment with taking risks, which helps them see themselves as powerful and competent.

The Outdoors Belongs to Everyone

The sky, the clouds, the rain, the sun, and the wind are for everyone equally to enjoy, as are the birds and insects. Watching and listening to these living creatures lift our spirits. Spending many hours in a classroom with other children and adults can lead to a sense of being confined; going outside can quickly energize and excite.

Being Outdoors Connects Children to the Community

Outdoors, children see and hear things in the community happen, change, and grow. Outdoors is where fire trucks scream and race, cranes dig deep holes to make room for new buildings, neighbors shop in a bodega, buses pick up and drop off passengers, farmers and gardeners plant and reap crops, bridges cross water. It is where a group of young children learns to cross streets while walking in the neighborhood, visit the pet store to buy food for the class fish, and stop at the grocery store to ask for empty boxes to turn into cars or boats. Outdoors is where children meet their neighbors who live next door or down the lane or on a different floor of their apart-

Stories From the Field: Facilitating Parent Involvement in Children's Gardening

Each year Farmer John comes to rototill the soil and construct long, straight rows covered for planting. As he works, he stops to speak to the children and answer questions. Once the rows are made, the children are eager to gather their seedlings and begin planting.

The Learning Garden is a part of our curriculum, and our class is involved in all aspects of choosing seeds, planting, tending, harvesting, and cooking the vegetables. The children are engaged and passionate about growing vegetables. Although the children were excited to share the discovery of a new plant growing, we noticed that their parents hesitated to pick green beans or smell the sunflowers. They were not entering the garden with their children. Instead they would stand and wait for their child at the front of the garden.

Because the garden beds were wide, parents could not walk over them. To enter the garden, they needed to walk down long 90-foot rows. On damp days or watering days, the ground between the rows became muddy.

We decided to redesign our garden space to be more inviting and easier to navigate. First, the construction of raised beds allowed us to have the area between the beds become hard grass surfaces, eliminating the muddy surfaces between garden beds. The beds in the front are arranged in a radial pattern reflecting the sunflowers we grow each year. The middle two beds create a welcoming flower tunnel that invites people to enter the garden. This leads families to a gazebo with seating in the middle of the space. The radial design also creates triangles that support agricultural play spaces for the children such as a corn maze, pumpkin patch, bean tipis, and a sunflower house. The back rows are short and straight to provide enough space for growing and engagement with a cucumber tunnel. Teachers also keep small bags on hand if families want to harvest vegetables for dinner.

Finding a solution was vital for the inclusion of parents—to develop our community and to develop diverse relationships.

—Beth Hallett, early childhood teacher, Child Study and Development Center at the University of New Hampshire and coordinator, Growing a Green Generation project

ment. It is where children feel brave or scared about a dog they see being walked on a leash. Depending on the neighborhood, children may be lucky enough to say hello to people of different ages, people of different ethnicities, and people who live in a variety of family situations. All of this gives children a sense of their own place in their families, in their neighborhoods, and in their communities. When children are always inside their school and

homes and vehicles, they miss out on such experiences. Pyle's phrase "the extinction of experience" applies here (1993, 145).

Being Outdoors Encourages Children to Develop a Love and Respect for Nature

Children need firsthand experiences to build on their innate biophilia—their bond with nature. They can learn a great deal of interesting information about their world from books and other media, but their understanding of and respect for the natural world is enhanced significantly through opportunities to dig in the dirt, pick dandelions, wipe the dew off leaves, chase squirrels around a tree, or watch birds congregate on a telephone wire. Teachers help children develop a love of nature by observing and sharing children's outdoor interests and building on what they know or feel. Environmentally minded adults typically trace their interest in the environment to a person from their childhoods who shared an appreciation of nature with them (Chawla 2006). The next generation of stewards for the earth is in our classrooms now, open to deepening their connection with nature.

Fifty years ago, families and educators could take for granted that young children would spend time outdoors (Clements 2004). Because children now spend less time outdoors, there is a greater consideration of the benefits of being outdoors and a deepening, widespread concern among educators for children who lack outdoor experiences (Children and Nature Network & IUCN Commission on Education and Communication 2012).

Research Supports the Importance of Nature for Young Children and Adults

In the last 20 years, an international research effort has confirmed what environmentalists, nature lovers, and early childhood educators have long believed: Nature is good for people. Rigorous, controlled research has made

The Relationship Between Nature and Human Health		
Dimension of health	More nature results in	Less nature results in
Social functioning	People are more generous and want to connect with others Stronger neighborhood ties, sense of community, more mutual trust and wanting to help one another More sharing of common spaces	Higher rates of aggression, violence, violent crime, and property crime— even after controlling for income and other differences More evidence of loneliness More individuals reporting inadequate social support
Psychological functioning	**Better cognitive functioning** More proactive, more effective patterns of life functioning **More self-discipline and impulse control** Greater mental health overall **Greater resilience in response to stressful life events**	**Exacerbated attention deficit/hyperactivity disorder symptoms** **More sadness and higher rates of clinical depression** More prone to stress and anxiety as shown in pulse rate, blood pressure, stress related patterns of nervous system and endocrine system anxiety, as well as physician-diagnosed anxiety disorders
Physical health	Enhanced recovery from surgery Enable and support more physical activity Improve immune system functioning Help diabetics achieve healthier blood glucose levels Improve functional health status and independent living skills among older adults	**Greater rates of childhood obesity** Higher rates of 15 out of 24 categories of physician-diagnosed diseases, including cardiovascular diseases Higher rates of mortality in young and older adults

Source: Adapted with permission from F.E. (Ming) Kuo, "Parks and Other Green Environments: Essential Components of a Healthy Human Habitat," Executive Summary (Ashburn, VA: National Recreation and Park Association, 2010), 2. www.nrpa.org/uploadedFiles/nrpa.org/Publications_and_Research/Research/Papers/MingKuo-Summary.PDF.

the case for nature in everyday life for everyone. Frances Kuo, a key scientific scholar in this area, summarized the strongest, most rigorous studies in a 2010 report for the National Recreation and Park Association, which is adapted for the box "The Relationship Between Nature and Human Health" on this page. "Nature" includes parks, views of trees and other vegetation, woods, fields, bits of green environments, yards, neighborhoods, and common outdoor spaces. Indicators particularly relevant to children are in bold type.

Features of Natural Environments That Support Children's Resilience and Strengths

Feature	Results
Natural surroundings and views of nature	Better concentration Better ability to inhibit impulses and delay gratification Better coping with upsetting events
Special place in nature	Opportunities to assimilate and transform experiences in places that are responsively alive Opportunities to feel connected to the larger universe of living things Memories that form a reservoir of calm to draw upon Familiarity with nature as a favorite place that can be recreated in new places
Nature play	Better concentration, ability to stay on task Better motor coordination and agility More cooperative, creative social play
Animal companions	A feeling of acceptance by a responsive, nonjudgmental creature
Animal care	Better self-control Better social skills
Gardening	Greater self-understanding Greater self-esteem Better interpersonal skills and ability to work in groups Increased sense of connection and responsibility to the environment

Source: Adapted from L. Chawla, "The Importance of Access to Nature for Young Children," *Early Childhood Matters* (June 2012): 50. http://vps.earlychildhoodmagazine.org/wp-content/uploads/2012/07/ECM118_11_The-importance-of-access-to-nature_Louise-Chawla.pdf.

Researchers have also identified particular features of natural environments that help children thrive. Louise Chawla, an international scholar of children's environments, has summarized this literature (2012); see the box "Features of Natural Environments That Support Children's Resilience and Strengths" on this page. Chawla's summary points to a developing area in the research—that of spiritual connecting to nature by young children. Her category of "special places" refers to this connection. See Chapter 4 on page 57 for more on research on spiritual connections shown by children.

The journal *Children, Youth and Environments* has published research on children and the outdoors since the 1980s. The journal is part of the

Children, Youth and Environments Center for Community Engagement at the University of Colorado, Boulder, which offers online access to the journal as well as a large database of images for scholars and planners (see www.colorado.edu/journals/cye/). The most comprehensive research reviews are available at the Children and Nature Network website (see www.childrenandnature.org). Useful selections from the yearly reviews are summarized in "Children and Nature Worldwide: An Exploration of Children's Experiences of the Outdoors and Nature With Associated Risks and Benefits" (Children and Nature Network & IUCN Commission on Education and Communication 2012).

Barriers to Outdoor Play

Despite these and other research findings showing the benefits and importance of outdoor play, barriers to providing children outdoor opportunities remain. Safety concerns, availability of space, pollution, busy family and school schedules, and an increase in screen time among children all limit children's outdoor exploration.

Concerns About Safety—Traffic

Traffic is one of the biggest barriers to children playing freely outdoors. Children have always played outside close to their home or early childhood setting, but roads for vehicles are dangerous barriers for people on foot. As Dargan and Zeitlin write, "The automobile gradually pushed children back from the streets—accident by accident, each one resulting in an outcry of protest against the drivers, but each inexorably changing the nature of play" (1990, 152). Roads and highways keep children isolated—from one another, from open spaces, from whatever is on the other side of the road. Young children are particularly limited in their explorations because sensible parents and teachers know that this age group's perceptions and judgments are no match for a vehicle's speed and momentum.

Furthermore, because families are concerned about children's safety when they play alone outside, they sometimes drive children to organized outdoor activities. This practice, typically part of suburban life, requires a lot of adult time, adds to traffic congestion, consumes gas and other resources, and keeps children underexercised and dependent on adults.

Cars, buses, and other vehicles take many of us out of our neighborhoods to work, attend school, and shop, and at the same time make us strangers in other families' neighborhoods. "It takes a village to raise a child," goes the African proverb, but in the United States many of the "villagers" are elsewhere and "strangers" are in our own villages. Children therefore have fewer opportunities to feel a part of their own communities.

Concerns About Safety—Stranger Danger Fear

In the late 1970s and early 1980s several tragic kidnappings led to the founding of the National Center for Missing and Exploited Children, which helped raise national awareness of potential dangers to children. Although only a small percentage of kidnappings in the United States are conducted by individuals unknown to the children involved, the possibility of one's child vanishing has made parents extremely cautious. As children get older, cautionary restrictions can affect their ability to independently explore the neighborhood; get to playgrounds, school, and the library; and visit shops and friends.

Being fearful of strangers in neighborhoods is an unfortunate aspect of our times. Adults need to work together to generate ways to restore community ties and allow children more freedom to plan and learn from their own outdoor activities and explorations.

More People, Less Play Space

As populations increase, more land is required for housing, workplaces, schools, and other services. Cities everywhere are growing, too often at the expense of green space. In addition, "disparities in park distribution are particularly evident in areas with low income and racial/ethnic populations" (National Recreation and Park Association 2011, iii). High-rise apartments create barriers between homes and the outdoors that make it difficult for young children to play outside, and densely inhabited streets often lack safe play spots. In some urban areas, negative social conditions, such as unemployment and homelessness, have made public spaces such as parks unsafe for children (Platt 2012). The American Public Health Association has recognized these realities and called for "nearby nature" as a public health necessity (APHA 2013).

Pollution and Environmental Justice

Pollution contributes to the deterioration of both natural and built areas and can be a deterrent to playing outdoors. Air pollution is a major contributor to the rising rates of asthma (Gammon 2012), which affects one of every 10 children and one of every six African American children. Air pollution may be linked to the development of autism as well (Roberts et al. 2013). Former

Administrator of the Environmental Protection Agency Lisa P. Jackson notes the uneven impact on certain populations,

> All too often, low-income, minority, and tribal Americans live in the shadows of the worst pollution, facing disproportionate health impacts and greater obstacles to economic growth in communities that cannot attract businesses and new jobs. (Office of Environmental Justice 2011, n.p.)

Although lead has been banned from use in gasoline and paint for years, it lingers in the soil in many older inner cities and manufacturing centers. In the last 40 years governments have made much progress in eradicating this poison, but nearly half a million children ages 1 to 5 years have elevated blood lead levels, and African American children are disproportionately affected (Centers for Disease Control and Prevention 2012a). For more on lead and other toxicants, see Chapter 3, "Precautions Outdoors."

Family Schedules Limit Outdoor Play

Today's families are busy. In 59 percent of families with young children, both parents work (US Bureau of Labor Statistics 2013). This results in parents often being away from home and children spending more time in child care programs, schools, and other group settings. Almost half of parents with preschoolers do not take them outside to play every day (Tandon, Zhou, & Christakis 2012). Even routine outdoor activities, such as walking to and from school, occur less frequently than in the past. The number of children walking to school declined from 68 percent in 1969 to 13 percent in 2009 (National Center for Safe Routes to School 2011).

The Loss of Recess

Recess for children in public kindergarten and primary grades started disappearing from schools in the 1980s. In part, growing pressure on teachers to ensure that children succeed academically has contributed to the limiting of outdoor play and recess in many programs and schools. However, in the last decade, concerns in the medical and public health communities about obesity and cardiovascular risk among children led to strong recommendations from national organizations and the federal government that children get at least 60 minutes per day of moderate to vigorous physical activity. The National Association for Sport and Physical Education (NASPE) recommends that elementary-age children have at least 20 minutes each day for recess, which is distinguished from physical education as "discretionary time" for children (2006). Many states do not make that distinction; in fact, some states do not require time for any physical activity during the school day (Bogden, Brizius, & Walker 2012).

The Screen Time Phenomenon

Television since the 1950s, video games and computers since the 1980s, and mobile devices since the 1990s have contributed to children's interest in spending more time indoors than out. Louv quotes a child as saying he wanted to play inside because "that's where the electrical outlets are" (2008, 10). Technology is here to stay. The challenge for adults who are concerned about children's development in all areas is to make sure children don't miss out on all the joys and benefits of being outdoors.

Given these daunting barriers, how can we ensure children's access to outdoor play and exploration? The next section outlines several hopeful directions.

National Response

The accumulation of high-quality research about the importance of outdoor play has spurred initiatives aimed at reconnecting children with natural environments.

Children and Nature Network

Richard Louv's bestselling *Last Child in the Woods,* first published in 2005, jangled a national nerve, and in 2007 Louv co-founded the Children and Nature Network (www.childrenandnature.org). The network collects research reports on children and nature and makes them available to anyone wishing to be an informed advocate. This has been invaluable to advancing the cause of children's access to the outdoors.

The network has also undertaken numerous initiatives to connect children to nature. It encourages families to form nature clubs with other families and has developed a helpful toolkit in English and Spanish on how to do so (see www.childrenandnature.org/downloads/NCFF_toolkit.pdf). The toolkit includes checklists for planning activities, issuing invitations and notices, making arrangements with parks, reminding families what to bring on expeditions, and more. The toolkit is an acknowledgment that many of today's parents may have missed out on nature experiences as children and now, as parents, need advice on making nature connections with their children.

The Children and Nature Network also offers

* A training program for young people, the Natural Leaders initiative
* The Natural Teachers Network for teachers

* A special fall initiative, Serve Outside September, involving multigenerational service projects
* Let's G.O.! (Get Outside), a youth-inspired, youth-led intergenerational initiative in April

The network collaborates with other nature-focused organizations and maintains a regional directory for the United States of more than one hundred collaborators, including campaigns, organizations, clubs, and other programs. Louv blogs about new research and initiatives and refers to the whole of the network's efforts as the New Nature Movement. His book *The Nature Principle* (2012) also supports the movement.

National Organizations

Nonprofit and professional organizations are also leading efforts to get children outdoors. The American Academy of Pediatrics (AAP), for example, advocates for outdoor play in numerous ways, even offering parents "prescriptions" for outdoor play. The Alliance for Childhood collaborated to sponsor the PBS documentary "Where Do the Children Play?" (and publishes an accompanying study guide) as well as the DVD "Wetlands and Wonder," produced by the Environmental Protection Agency (EPA). PBS also showcased a film on the relationship between children and nature, "Mother Nature's Child" (see www.mothernaturesmovie.com). Recognizing that recess is essential to children's physical, social, and academic development, NASPE (2006), as mentioned previously in this chapter, calls for a minimum of 20 minutes of recess per day for elementary students to help reverse the trend of schools eliminating recess from their schedules.

Organizations not primarily focused on children's issues recognize that childhood experiences in nature can lead to adult stewardship of nature (Chawla & Derr 2012). The National Wildlife Federation (NWF) is a prime example. With nearly four million members interested in protecting animals, the NWF recognized in the mid-1990s that its Backyard Habitat program could be extended to schoolyard habitats (Rivkin 1997). School habitats provide additional places for wildlife and encourage children to develop an interest in the natural world and become its stewards.

More recently, the NWF became a member of the international organization Eco-Schools, which sets standards for environmentally sound practices for schools ("green" schools) around the world (see www.nwf.org/Eco-Schools-USA.aspx). An essential feature of Eco-Schools is that children spend time outdoors *every day*. Early childhood teachers thinking about greening their schools might want to consider the Eco-Schools model. The NWF has strengthened its outreach to families with its Be Out There campaign, which offers well-developed publications and suggested activities to help families with young children have pleasurable, educational outdoor experiences.

The NWF, in collaboration with the Natural Learning Initiative, has also developed guidelines for groups and individuals wanting to create nature play spaces for children.

While the founding mission of the Arbor Day Foundation is to encourage planting and caring for trees, the organization has helped inspire the creation and maintenance of hundreds of nature play spaces, particularly at schools and centers. The Arbor Day Foundation collaborated with the Dimensions Educational Research Foundation to form Nature Explore, which conducts research on children and nature, provides design consultation for outdoor classrooms, publishes books and catalogs, and holds workshops and conferences for educators and others. Nature Explore also supplies materials for outdoor nature play spaces (see www.natureexplore.org).

Another well-established organization, the Nature Conservancy, operates in all states and 30 countries and works to protect large tracts of undeveloped land. The organization reaches young children and their families and teachers with the online program Nature Rocks, which offers information and activities particularly useful for families and teachers who may be unconnected to nature centers or clubs (see www.naturerocks.org). The Nature Conservancy also partners with the Children and Nature Network (see p. 14).

GreenHearts is a newer, smaller organization (see www.greenheartsinc.org). Its newsletter addresses thorny issues such as risky play (risk and hazard are not the same—children need some risk to grow) and natural items (sticks, leaves, flowers) children can play with in ways that will not hurt the natural area. The North American Association for Environmental Education (NAAEE) has launched the Natural Start Alliance, a network of organizations and agencies focused on early childhood outdoor education.

The Federal Government Response

Several federal government initiatives focus on encouraging children to be more active. First Lady Michelle Obama has demonstrated the importance of organic gardening with children, focusing on both the gardening experience and wholesome nutrition. Her vigorous Let's Move campaign has attracted many supporters and in 2012 contributed to the formation of the new Presidential Fitness Program. In 2011 the Department of Education developed the Green Ribbon Schools award, which honors schools demonstrating "reduced environmental impact and costs," "effective environmental and sustainability education," and "improved health and wellness," including "high standards of nutrition, fitness, and *quantity of quality outdoor time for both students and staff*" (emphasis added) (see www2.ed.gov/programs/green-ribbon-schools/eligibility.html).

In addition, in 2012 the EPA announced the formation of the Federal Interagency Task Force on Environmental Education, to be co-led by EPA and the Departments of Education and Interior. This novel interagency approach to environmental education is welcome.

Beginning in 2010 the National Park Service has undertaken a major effort with other nations called Healthy Parks, Healthy People. The Strategic

Action Plan (2011) outlines a far-reaching agenda of research, outreach, and collaboration that will make all parks cornerstones of sustainable healthy communities.

A New Nature Movement?

Louv's (2012) New Nature Movement encompasses all the activity discussed in this chapter. The movement seems to be emerging in response to climate change and to people feeling disconnected from nature. This movement goes beyond a focus on sustainability and conservation to one of building healthier relationships with the natural world and with other people. In the chapters that follow, we will look at early childhood settings and schools that are helping to shape that vision, challenges in the outdoor environment that teachers must be aware of, new work on how children's spiritual development informs the vision, and finally to the pressing reality of both the present and future —the growing population in cities and how we can keep nature accessible for children in the face of expanding urban areas.

Reflections

* What have I noticed around where I live?

* Is open space available for children? Do children use it?

* How good is my center's or school's space? What makes it good for children? How might I help change it to make it better?

What You Can Do

1. Talk with your colleagues—show them the research. Does anyone share your interest and concern?

2. Check the Children and Nature Network—it has a teacher support group.

3. Protest the erosion of space for children in your locality— you might not win but you will be putting the idea out there that children need nature.

2

Early Childhood Settings With Outdoors in Mind

A re you a teacher who takes children outdoors to connect with the natural environment? Children will remember these experiences, as Alexandra, a young teacher, shows in this account of her own experiences in second grade.

My second grade teacher often took our whole class to a park a few blocks away from the school. It had a big playground and was surrounded by lots of trees. A shallow creek ran between the playground and an open field. We brought containers and wore boots to go trudging through the creek, picking up pieces of trash as we explored the water. I remember being shocked at finding so many different kinds of trash, from plastic bags to candy wrappers to soda cans. It made me more aware of littering and its effect on nature and ecosystems, and it also made me more conscious of conservation efforts like recycling. We learned the difference between trash and recyclables and separated the two. This was a great introduction to conversations about the environment and the importance of preserving nature.

Besides the educational value of cleaning up the park, the activity provided a lot of positive memories and experiences connected to volunteering and nature. I remember holding on to my best friend when trying not to slip on the rocks in the stream—inevitably slipping and falling into the water and laughing with my friends as they helped me up. I remember a bee stinging my finger, and even though it hurt a lot, I also remember it fondly because it sparked a class discussion about bees, different kinds of bugs, and how to avoid or handle getting stung. It also helped me get over my fear of bees, and since then I have regarded them as creatures that will generally leave me in peace if I do the same. I recall walking through the neighborhood on the way to the park and my classmates pointing to their houses as we passed them. It resulted in playdates with peers I hadn't realized lived so close to me. It made me feel like part of a community, a neighborhood, a classroom family.

—Alexandra Alton

Just as Friedrich Froebel responded to changes within the family unit brought about by industrialization by establishing a "garden for children"—the kindergarten—contemporary educators in the United States and abroad have responded to the modern weakening of the child-nature link with an array of nature-focused schools and programs. The United Kingdom and the Scandinavian countries developed inspiring projects in the 1990s and continue to do so; there are also inspiring books on the subject by Americans, including Sharon Danks (2010), Rusty Keeler (2008), Eric Nelson (2012), and Nature Explore (2011).

The work of Robin Moore provided the foundation for the great flowering of nature-focused schools in the United States. He has led or contributed to projects across the country and added to the research confirming the value of outdoor play. Building on Wilson's biophilia hypothesis (Wilson 2008), Moore extended thinking in the field about the deep roots of humans' affinity for nature. He emphasized universal design (1992; Moore & Cosco 2007b) and shared his work through the Natural Learning Initiative (www.naturalearning.org). With Nilda Cosco, he developed an evaluation system for preschool play yards, a statewide project with Head Start programs, and a dozen Montessori outdoor settings (2007a). Public parks have received his input as well, in Chicago, Cincinnati, and New York, for example.

Biophilia

Biophilia is "the innate tendency to focus on life and lifelike processes" (Wilson 1984, 1). Human beings are attracted to life, to living things; we are bonded with them. It is a child snuggling with her dog, her open-mouth gaze of wonder at a butterfly, her gentle transferring of a ladybug from one finger to another. Biophilia is our link with other life (Kellert & Wilson 1993, 20).

Examples of Settings With Outdoors in Mind

While walking in the outdoor classroom, 4-year-old Derek finds in the ground a small evergreen-type plant. He picks it and brings it to his teacher, saying, "I know there is something like it."

Derek takes his teacher to the big evergreen tree and begins touching his plant to the needles on the tree. He looks back and forth between the two, comparing them closely.

With his plant in hand, Derek finds Xiangyu and Sef and tells them about his discovery. "Compare this leaf with those trees," he says. "I have to figure out how 'pokey' [having sharp points] my plant is. I think it's the same as this one [the pine tree]."

Derek keeps trying to sort things out, saying, "I know something around here is just like this plant." For the rest of his time outside, he looks at various plants to find the perfect match. (Gerdes & Miller 2011, 27)

Enduring Traditions: Steiner, Montessori, and Dewey

Froebel's nineteenth-century kindergarten is the basis for nature-based schools, but Rudolf Steiner, Maria Montessori, and John Dewey also helped develop the nature-based tradition.

Steiner's Waldorf schools. Rudolf Steiner's Waldorf schools began in the early twentieth century and have been established around the world as well as in the United States. Steiner believed that beauty, simplicity, and order support young children's development. Thus Waldorf early childhood settings bring nature into the classroom for observation and play. They are filled with simple, natural materials and objects, such as wood, wool, stones, sticks, shells, pinecones, soft cotton dolls, and wooden animals. Children experience the natural world, not a manufactured one, to appreciate its beauty and rhythms.

Each classroom has a table or other area where seasonal objects are carefully displayed and refreshed (Fenner & Rivers 1992; van Leeuwen & Moeskops 2008). Children celebrate the seasons and their associated holidays and events; songs, stories, and poetry about nature are part of the day. Teachers tell the children stories and poems rather than read to them to help children develop their memory and foster their own ideas. The natural world is animate, and children use it as a source of imagination—fairies,

---

Universal Design

Universal design is an evolving set of principles that guide the process of making schools and other buildings, playgrounds, parks, and the rest of the built environment suitable, accessible, and enjoyable for everyone. Universal design focuses attention on diversity in gender, ethnicity, socioeconomic status, age, physical and mental ability/disability, and religion, in "the multiple realism of design—media, product, architectural, and urban design" (Ostroff 2011, 17). Universal design also applies to curriculum design and practices.

elves, and flower babies may be topics of conversation. The furniture in Waldorf classrooms is made from wood, toys are stored in wicker baskets, and lightweight silk cloths drape over wooden playstands to make houses. Children participate in making their snacks from basic ingredients: bread made from wheat grains that they grind into flour, oatmeal from freshly milled oat grains, fresh and dried fruit, or fresh vegetables grown outside if practical. Children learn that their food comes from things that have grown outdoors.

Children go outside every day, with families expected to provide appropriate clothing for the weather conditions. Like the indoor classroom, the outdoor environment is based on natural elements, with gardens if possible and objects such as tree stumps, logs, and pinecones for the children to use in their play. A tree or logs provide climbing experiences. Teachers take care of the outdoor environment by raking, sweeping, and planting. Just as children learn to play "school" by what they typically experience indoors, they learn to care for nature and the outdoors by watching and imitating the teachers. Expeditions to the world beyond the play yard enable children to experience the local area. For more information on contemporary Waldorf schooling, see Nicol and Taplin (2012).

Montessori. Maria Montessori, a contemporary of Steiner, noted that humankind "belongs to nature, and, especially when he is a child, he must draw from it the forces necessary to the development of the body and of the spirit. We have intimate communications with nature which have an influence, even a material influence, on the growth of the body" (1912 [1964], 153). Montessori described how "agriculture and animal culture contain in themselves precious means of moral education" (156). By caring for plants and animals in the early childhood setting, children

* Learn to observe living things and the effects of the children's care on them

* Develop foresight by realizing that without their care, living things may suffer

* Develop "patience and . . . confident expectation, which is a form of faith and a philosophy of life" (159)

* Are "inspired with a feeling of nature, which is maintained by the marvels of creation" (159)

Montessori's first Children's House in Rome had a large courtyard cultivated as a garden, with trees, a path, and a long stretch divided into garden plots for each child 4 years and older. The younger children were free to explore the courtyard. The school also raised chickens, rabbits, and pigeons.

Montessori, like Steiner, continues to inspire early childhood educators. In a public charter Montessori school in inner-city Baltimore, for example, the former asphalt parking lot now has a vegetable garden, a beehive, a chicken coop, and a butterfly garden.

Another urban Montessori school, housed in a storefront on a major thoroughfare in Washington, DC, backs up to the lush woods of Rock Creek Park. Children visit the park regularly led by a nature specialist, Amy Beam. Amy is keenly knowledgeable about the ecology of the park, perhaps a necessity given the lack of localized nature training in typical preschool education. This school can be seen in the video "Where Do the Children Play?" This Montessori school is an adaptation of Montessori's idea—there is no room for a school yard so the woods suffices to teach about nature.

Dewey. John Dewey believed that nature should be the unifying theme for educating young children: "When we think that we all live on the earth, that we live in an atmosphere, that our lives are touched at every point by the influences of the soil, flora, and fauna, by considerations of light and heat," we realize that education should be directly connected to the real world (1900/1902 [1990], 76). Dewey envisioned the ideal school as having "about it a natural environment. It ought to be in a garden, and the children from the garden would be led on to surrounding fields, and then into the wider country, with all its facts and forces" (75). Since young children are mostly interested in their immediate world, he discussed the role of food as a starting point for science education:

> All the materials that come into the kitchen have their origin in the country; they have come from the soil, are nurtured through the influences of light and water, and represent a great variety of local environments. Through this connection, extending from the garden to the larger world, the child has his most natural introduction to the study of the sciences. Where did these things grow? What was necessary to their growth? . . . and so on. (83)

In reaction to the dry, abstract, textbook-based curriculum of the time, Dewey's insistence on nature as the basis for children's learning still informs education and is an underpinning for nature center preschools.

No One Has Fun When They Are Cold: Clothes for the Outdoors

As we get closer to colder weather, we want to prepare you for what will be appropriate attire for playing outdoors. For those of you new to the preschool, we convert the hill down to the swings into a sledding hill; we have snowshoes that are just the right size, and winter is so much fun when we can discover it together outdoors. We believe that there's no such thing as bad weather, just bad equipment. The more comfortable your child is, the more he or she will enjoy exploring the frozen forest, discovering various animal tracks, and finding spots where the squirrels have dug through the snow to excavate some hidden treasure.

When temperatures reach 40 degrees or less, a second layer on your child's legs and mittens or gloves on your child's hands would help them stay warm enough. When in doubt, dress in layers. As soon as there is snow on the ground, children should have waterproof snow pants or a snowsuit. Waterproof mittens are better than gloves to keep their little hands warm. Rain boots are not warm enough once the weather is colder than 25 degrees. Heads should be covered once the temperature reaches 35 degrees or less; hats tend to keep people the warmest.

Keep in mind that children grow quickly and may even grow out of winter gear by mid-February. If you need any assistance with clothing, please let us know. Gear is available to borrow at the preschool. You may also consider donating gear your children have outgrown for others to use.

We would like children to be as independent as possible with getting their outdoor clothing on and off. Slip-on boots without laces makes it easier for them to feel independent. Snowsuits tend to be easier than snow pants and a jacket.

Thank you for helping make your children's outdoor time more enjoyable for them!

—Christine Lambert, Oak Room Teacher

Reprinted, by permission, from C. Lambert, *The DragonFly* (Dodge Nature Preschool newsletter, Fall/Winter 2010): 7. www.dodgenaturecenter.org.

Nature Center Preschools

Nature centers protect natural surroundings and invite the public to explore the wonders of the outdoors. Nature centers have increasingly added preschool education to their programming, using their grounds for teaching and exploration. Consider the following examples of nature center preschools.

Dodge Nature Preschool. A particularly beautiful preschool is at the Thomas Irvine Dodge Nature Center in St. Paul, Minnesota. Situated on 110 acres of woodland and meadows, the center includes a model farm, beehives, fruit trees, and flower and vegetable gardens. The center offers preschoolers a wide range of experiences with nature (in the winter, for example, children help tap trees and collect sap that will be used to make maple syrup). The preschool building, trimmed and furnished with local wood, was especially designed for young children. Each classroom has a door to the large outdoor play area. Low, wide windows enable children to see the outdoors at all times. Child-size binoculars, stuffed play birds, bird guides, and children's books about birds encourage children to observe the outdoor environment. Bird feeders attract a variety of birds year round. A painting easel is located near the window along with many art supplies.

Children go outdoors every day for long hikes and playtimes. Families are expected to provide suitable clothing for the Minnesota weather (see the box "No One Has Fun When They Are Cold"). Children gather outdoor materials—leaves, stones, sticks, blossoms—to use in their play and projects. Both teachers and children initiate projects, and the curriculum flows from the teachers' and children's interests.

Schlitz Audubon Nature Preschool. Another preschool rich with nature experiences is the Schlitz Audubon Nature Preschool, located on 185 acres in suburban Milwaukee. Here children begin the day with outdoor play, sunshine or snow. On one snowy morning I saw the children digging, making snow angels, damming runoff from melting snow, climbing on stones, and climbing the perimeter fences. Later they headed inside for group time and a wide choice of nature-themed activities for individuals or small groups, then back outside they went. On this day they walked to a woodland area with stick bridges, stones, bushes, trees, and creeks that had formed from the melting snow. Although the yard was fenced, the impression was of being in the open snowy woods.

Children go outdoors every day, often hiking in the woods and on the Lake Michigan beach. In the winter, winds blow the lake water into huge frozen mounds on the shore, creating interior spaces—ice caves—that the children explore. The indoor classroom offers children many materials from the outdoors and tools for studying them—binoculars, magnifying glasses, aquariums, and cages.

Other nature preschools. The New Canaan Nature Preschool in Connecticut is the oldest such program in the country, founded in 1967. New Canaan has a conventional playground, but children explore the woods and marshes daily.

The preschool has a well-articulated policy on the value of nature for children:

> The . . . nature preserve is your child's classroom and playground. . . . Nature as the venue is the best the world can offer these young children, and these experiences in these early years will last a lifetime. (New Canaan Nature Center Preschool 2012)

Other well-established nature preschools include the Nature Preschool at Chippewa Nature Center and the Nature's Way Preschool at Kalamazoo Nature Center, both in Michigan. The Massachusetts Audubon Society conducts the second oldest nature preschool, Arcadia, and another one at Drumlin Farm. There is a preschool at Irvine Nature Center near Baltimore. As of 2012 there are 20-plus nature center preschools, with more planned (Bailie 2012). Larimore (2011), drawing on her experience founding the center at Chippewa, offers an accessible how-to guide on establishing such preschools.

Nature center preschools have tremendous resources for nature-centered education: spacious grounds and uniquely qualified teachers, who typically have backgrounds in both environmental education and early childhood education. Chippewa, Dodge, Schlitz, and Irvine have used these resources to benefit children and also to sponsor teacher trainings and conferences to share their knowledge.

Immersion in the Outdoors—An American Forest School

The late Anita Rui Olds, a brilliant and compassionate child care center designer, wrote in 2001, "The original playscapes—before day care centers and playgrounds—were the fields, woods, paths, and streams near children's homes. Through experience with nature's wonders in the form of sand, water, mud, trees, rocks, bushes, worms, children received all the necessary motor stimulation" (411). Erin Kenny, a former lawyer and now ethnobotanist/early childhood teacher and director, has revived those playscapes at Cedarsong Nature School on Vashon Island in the state of Washington. At Cedarsong, located on a secluded five-acre site in the lightly populated woods in the center of the island, at the end of a narrow dirt road, 2- to 6-year-old children spend several hours a day playing and learning in the mossy, ferny, evergreen forest. (See www.cedarsongnatureschool.org or read Kenny's 2013 book *Forest Kindergartens: The Cedarsong Way*.)

Children stay outdoors the entire time at Cedarsong. They are appropriately dressed. The teachers give families guidance on clothes that are appropriate for long periods of time in the outdoors. One functional building serves as storage only; the children do not go inside.

On the day I visited the program, there was a large muddy puddle to "fish" in with whatever sticks could be found, and a stick bridge to march over the puddle on. Because the temperature was about 33 degrees, children were discouraged from wading in the big puddle or jumping off the bridge until it was close to the time when their parents were about to come. Better to stay dry-footed and dry-legged than wet and cold for two or three hours. Meanwhile, children had logs to climb, bushes to hide under, rocks and leaves to find, birds to listen for and imitate, and a snack from the teachers to enjoy.

The children enjoyed a hot potato, a very good snack in the cold weather (both to hold and eat). The teacher brought a big thermos of hot water and placed some tasty leaves in it before snack time so everyone could enjoy "forest tea" in small cups. Then the children set off for more exploration and rediscoveries of favorite places. The children and teachers sang some songs about nature. Erin and her co-teacher commented on things they or the children observed, using the "Rachel Carson manner" of talking and wondering about plants, bird songs, or some change in the flora and fauna without pressuring children to also make comments.

In the woods around Cedarsong, the children have named paths, clearings, and puddles. Everything is available for exploration and handling. Some manufactured items help with this—plastic cups for pouring, plastic buckets for transporting, plastic magnifying glasses for investigating—all things that won't rust in the persistently damp evergreen woods. Erin has developed other practical strategies over the years. The school's policy on sticks, for example, takes safety seriously but also reflects the fact that sticks are beloved by children and historically have been used as tools by people all over the world. (See sidebar.)

> ### Cedarsong Guidance on Sticks
> In children's fertile imagination, a stick can be a wand, a kite, an umbrella, a horse to ride, or a digging tool. Instead of forbidding children to carry, swing, or throw sticks, I build in safety rules. Children are told to carry sticks with the point to the ground, that large sticks must be parked outside of enclosed spaces like their forest huts, and that throwing is only permitted into the forest and away from the group. Likewise, sticks are never to be used against another child as a weapon. I give the children specific areas and opportunities to throw sticks at designated targets. (Kenny 2013, 15)

Though children's intuitive interactions with nature can at times worry adults, they are a natural part of learning about the world. The spirit of the place supports the spirit of the child, as Chapter 4 illustrates. So instead of saying no to picking up sticks and throwing stones and picking berries, Cedarsong teachers validate children's interests and actions and offer guidance. Cedarsong also provides teacher training and Therapeutic Nature Immersion programs, one for families and one for children with autism or attention-deficit/hyperactivity disorder (ADHD). These programs help participants to more deeply connect with one another, nature, and their own selves.

International Forest Schools

The American schools noted in the previous section are privately funded and offer part-time programs. Some British forest schools combine private and public funding to run their part-time programs. In contrast, forest schools in Denmark and Germany are typically publicly funded, which allows for more supplies, greater programming support (such as buses for transportation), and the possibility of additional professionally trained teachers. A more general discussion of forest schools appears in "What Are Forest Schools?" (NAEYC 2011).

The United Kingdom. The United Kingdom has numerous forest schools that supplement children's regular school programming. Typically meeting once a week or during vacations, children participate in activities and explore in wooded settings. An international leader in the forest school movement, Claire Warden, has written extensively about this educational experience—see, for example, *Nature Kindergartens and Forest Schools: An Exploration of Naturalistic Learning Within Nature Kindergartens and Forest Schools* (2012).

Denmark. The forest schools in Denmark are child care centers. The Danish central government guarantees every child a space in a child care center from 6 months until school age (6–7 years old). Thus, child care is virtually universal and central to childrearing. Parents and the well-trained, professional child care staff regard each other as partners and share the responsibility for children's development. Offering a homelike, informal atmosphere, the Danish centers aim to provide a happy life for children. Outside experiences at forest schools are varied and wide ranging and include gardening, tending farm animals, and play in adjoining meadows and forests. Children engage in woodworking and other crafts using real tools, including knives for supervised whittling. In the dark Northern winter, fire pits are a regular feature. Staff at schools that value forest play but lack space take the children to woodland areas in buses. Williams-Siegfredsen (2012) provides a more complete description of Danish forest schools. The Danish forest schools present a wonderful model for child care centers—fully funded programs, fully engaged families, and a goal of a happy childhood.

Germany. German forest schools are also child care based. Schäffer and Kistemann's (2012) study of 12 German forest kindergartens observed that 2- to 6-year-old children were outside at least three hours every day, hiked to their play area for the day, and ate both breakfast and lunch in the forest. Several different natural environments were available. Beginning and ending rituals framed the day, with the time between spent in free play in the natural environment. A handcart was pulled to the sites with materials for children's use: "craft materials, penknives, saws, magnifiers, ropes, spare clothes, books to read to the children, field guides for flora and fauna, etc." (275). The authors observed high levels of cooperation, communication, and creativity among the children. Children played across age levels. Teachers in these schools followed the children's interests, expanding on their observations and facilitating their learning. Families were very supportive of the forest schools and often helped start them.

Eco-Early Childhood Education

Starting in the early 1990s, South Korean educators created a new paradigm called eco-early childhood education, which "proposes moving from child- to life-centered, individual- to community-centered, and cognitive- to body, mind, and spirit-centered early childhood education" (Kim & Lim 2007, 42). Elements of an eco-early childhood education program include walking, meditation, vegetable gardening, handicrafts, traditional Korean physical exercise, temperance and saving (learning to reuse and recycle), food programs (cooking and eating organic, seasonal food), interaction between elders and children, and interchange between urban and rural communities. For more on eco-early childhood education in South Korea, see Kim and Lim 2007.

Schoolyard Habitats and Green Schools

In the 1990s the National Wildlife Federation (NWF) extended its popular Backyard Habitat program to schools with the Schoolyard Habitats program. Teachers and children of all ages learn how to develop outdoor areas for native birds, insects, and aquatic life. This benefits not only the wildlife but also the children, who gain a better understanding of the natural world and a wide variety of skills through creating and maintaining the habitats. Good habitats for animals are also good for children (Rivkin 1997). The program is now international.

A Schoolyard Habitat can be very modest—for example, a pot of zinnias and lantana as a nectar source for butterflies can give a program or class a way to start adding nature to its yard. The NWF website offers numerous

Stories From the Field: Winter Weather in Outdoor Classrooms

Dealing with winter weather in outdoor classrooms is one of the challenges I've encountered in our own research classrooms at Dimensions Foundation, and in the organizations we support through our Nature Explore Program. As often happens in life, however, this challenge turned out to be a great opportunity in disguise. One of our education specialists, Heather Fox, reached out to our network of Certified Nature Explore Classrooms to ask teachers what they do to engage children in outdoor winter learning. What emerged is a list of "top five" suggestions for inspiring children to celebrate winter that Heather shared on a blog post (see http://natureexplorecommu-nity.org/2014/natures-icebox-4-tips-for-play-in-a-cold-weather-outdoor-classroom/).

When children are encouraged to explore outdoor classrooms every day, they develop a personal understanding of the seasons. Here are five tips that encourage exploration and discovery in the outdoor classroom should your seasons include a winter wonderland.

Saunter Like a Snowflake

Have you ever wondered how a snowflake might feel as it dances through the air? Take advantage of the winter weather, step outside, and experience it. Invite children to mimic what they observe about snowflakes and joyfully participate in movement exploration. Use questions to help guide children to use their whole bodies to communicate what they know and feel.

Ask: "What might you look like if you were a snowflake?"

Melting Mosaics

Winter landscapes are less colorful than spring or fall. Create some color and experience the effect of melting with this activity. Combine salt and tempera paint to create a colorful melting mixture. Allow the children to explore the properties of snow and ice as they paint with the mixture. Encourage the children to use many words to describe what they are seeing.

Tool Tutorial

Get out your child-size tools and help children use them. Snow and ice create a different medium and a new challenge for children. This type of heavy work can help ground and focus the children's attention. The movement also keeps them warm and healthy.

Illuminating Ice

Freeze natural items like seedpods or berries in containers of clear water. Pop out the frozen creations and string nature's beauty from the trees in your outdoor classroom. Ask children to observe the ways in which the birds and animals react to your creations. Encourage them to notice how the sun shines through and to sketch what they see.

Recycled Trees

Try adding already cut evergreen trees (recycled Christmas trees perhaps?) to your outdoor classroom's messy materials area. Encourage children to build forts, design their own pathways, and discover trees from an entirely different perspective.

—Nancy Rosenow, executive director, Dimensions Foundation/Nature Explore, and Heather Fox, education specialist

resources for teachers (www. nwf.org/Get-Outside/Outdoor-Activities/Garden-for-Wildlife/Schoolyard-Habitats/). As mentioned in Chapter 1, the NWF is also a partner in the international Eco-Schools program, which helps schools teach environmentally responsible behavior across the school day, from use of resources (lighting, water, energy) to recycling to stewardship of the natural environment (both the school grounds and surroundings).

The Eco-School program is similar to the Green Schools National Network in the United States, with the exception that in the Eco-Schools program children must go outside every day. The Green Schools movement began in several places in the United States, including Maryland, which has had a program since 1998 (Rivkin 2011). In 2012 the Green Schools National Network held its second annual national conference, and later that year the US Department of Education gave out Green Ribbon Schools awards to schools that met three criteria for environmentally protective practices: "reduced environmental impact and costs, improved health and wellness, and effective environmental education" (US Department of Education 2012). For the improved health and wellness criterion, outdoor play/experience is required. Private and public pre-K–12 schools and school districts are eligible for the awards. The program is distinguished by unusual levels of collaboration among federal agencies, particularly the Environmental Protection Agency (EPA) and the Departments of Agriculture, Interior, and Energy. Another group of interest is the new International School Grounds Alliance (www.greenschoolyards. org), which has held two international conferences. (See the video "Voices From the International School Grounds Movement.") The Canadian foundation Evergreen, a proponent of school greening since the 1990s, is prominent in the International School Grounds Alliance.

Connecting to the Outdoors

The primary intent of American nature center preschools is to provide children more contact with nature. Other types of early childhood settings may view nature more instrumentally—using the outdoors and nature to teach science or stewardship of the earth, for example. For administrative purposes, some teachers may feel they have to justify taking children outside by connecting outdoor activities to the program's goals and objectives.

What Are Loose Parts?
In a preschool, loose parts are materials that can be moved, carried, combined, redesigned, lined up, and taken apart and put back together in multiple ways. They are materials with no specific set of directions that can be used alone or combined with other materials. (Kable 2010)

Many preschools have flexible schedules and can experiment with adding outdoor time. For example, one large center in Maryland offered a morning-only preschool class that spent at least an hour a day outdoors, in most weather conditions. Teacher Lori Biamonte emailed families daily with photos and comments about what the children learned, for example, as they leaped from a mulch pile. It was striking that only the outdoor class felt the need to explain its activities. But it was also striking that when the director announced the class, parents quickly enrolled their children, and a waiting list soon developed. The teachers and parents worked to expand what the outdoor space offered the children, and new loose parts—materials that can be used in different ways and in various combinations—kept materializing. The more the teachers explained to parents the clever and interesting things their children were doing, the more the parents found ways to extend the experiences their children were interested in.

A Place to Start: Better Play Yards

Nature-focused preschool programs greatly enrich children's development. However, given what we know about the benefits of outdoor play, a child who is in a center for perhaps 50 hours a week for 50 weeks a year with minimal nature experience could be considered underserved. Similarly, a child in kindergarten or grade school with an inadequate yard is also underserved. To better meet children's needs, we should view nature play yards as essential as literacy, art, and other centers are. How can this be accomplished?

When we consider children's experiences outdoors—observing the sky and clouds and sometimes a pale partial moon, letting the wind hit their faces and hands, feeling the rain or snow falling on their heads and outstretched hands, sniffing smells that are nice (or not), listening to the sounds of birds or people or motors, exploring rough and smooth textures under their shoes—we might concede that all these outdoor experiences are good, perhaps essential, for children. But observing a young child's deep interest and pleasure in climbing a tree, picking dandelions, or chasing a butterfly compels us to say, yes, living things *must* be available to children. Once in an old Victorian school yard in urban England, a child was showing me its features—sandbox, little hill, tetherball, and so on. "And that," he said, pointing to a 20-foot strip of grass backed by a row of shrubs and a high brick wall, "that is our *wilderness.*" It doesn't take much living nature to stir children, but it does take something.

The main requirement for adding living nature to play yards is belief in its importance. If you look at a fenced, mowed, and mulched play space with brightly colored commercial equipment and think there must be something more compelling for children, you can begin a transformation! Think about what would be fun for children, would change over time, would offer mystery—"places to play, toys to find and create, nooks and dens to hide in, tiny (or not-so-tiny) animals to pursue, and quiet sanctuaries for daydreaming or talking with a friend" (Bailie & Finch forthcoming). There are many resources available for inspiration.

A good place to start might be to consider the ongoing work begun years ago by Robin Moore's partners at MIG, an environment design firm, in their stunning transformation of a smallish parking lot at Tule Elk Park. A child care center that is part of the San Francisco Unified School District, Tule Elk Park features vine-covered fences, a stage, storage cabinet, raised vegetable gardens, compost, a small wooded area, trees, lavish flower beds, bike paths, a play house, an art room, a place for sand play, and even some conventional play equipment. Both *Asphalt to Ecosytems: Design Ideas for Schoolyard Transformation* (Danks 2010) and *How to Grow a School Garden* (Bucklin-Sporer & Pringle 2010) have numerous photos of Tule Elk. More photos of this pioneering urban site are at www.tuleelkpark.org.

Asphalt to Ecosytems is an excellent source of ideas for adding nature to outdoor play areas, as is Rusty Keeler's *Natural Playscapes: Creating Outdoor Play Environments for the Soul* (2008). Both have numerous photos from yards in the United States and abroad. Danks's work with many public schools in the San Francisco Bay Area has given her an understanding of school regulations and preferences. Eric Nelson also has many photographs in *Cultivating Outdoor Classrooms: Designing and Implementing Child-Centered Learning Environments* (2012). Nature Explore has a comprehensive array of useful, accessible publications, including *Learning With Nature Idea Book: Creating Nurturing Outdoor Spaces for Children* (2007), *Growing With Nature: Supporting Whole-Child Learning in Outdoor Classrooms* (2011), and *Keeping It Growing: Sustaining Your Outdoor Classroom* (2012).

Some local, state, and regional governments provide resources on how to transform school yards. Maryland, for instance, offers a toolkit for developing school yard habitats from the Maryland Association for Environmental and Outdoor Education, US Fish and Wildlife Service, and the NOAA Bay Watershed Education and Training Program (Schoolyard Habitat Partnership 2010) and guidelines from the state department of education for using school courtyards (Maryland State Department of Education 2012). A national reference for safety is the US Consumer Product Safety Commission's (CPSC) *Public Playground Safety Handbook* (2010), which includes such information as the type and depth of shock absorbent materials that should be used on areas of the playground where children are climbing.

Guidelines for play yards. The best general guidelines for creating inviting outdoor environments for children are offered by Bill Lucas of the United Kingdom's pioneering Learning Through Landscapes movement, which began in the 1990s. He notes four items basic to a school yard worthy of children (1994):

* Places to sit
* Shade
* Water
* Native flora and fauna—these are the children's heritage

This list is a good place to start. Other ideas for outdoor play spaces include pathways, signs, natural artwork, and places to dig, dance, run, and hide. Consider also the following suggestions.

* Landscape with native species (trees, shrubs, flowers, and grass) so that the plants will thrive and support native creatures and so that children will learn the types of living things that belong in their area (Tallamy 2009). Many nurseries have excellent selections of native plants. Consider the play value of plants—for instance, do they have pods, cones, or abundant blossoms that children can handle and investigate and use in their play (Moore 1993)?

* Use native logs and rocks in landscaping when possible. Exploring how the different barks and rocks feel offers children valuable sensory experiences. Sue Humphries at Coombes School in England had boulders trucked in from every part of the island so children could explore the differences between them. Use native sand in sandboxes if obtainable, and provide materials for digging and making mud (see Jan White's *Making a Mud Kitchen* (2012) for a delightful way for children to explore the dirt under their feet). When children use all their senses to explore the basic elements of the land, the information they gain contributes to their understanding of the flora and fauna in their environment.

* Plant a vegetable garden. Keep in mind that if your program closes in the summer, plants are not likely to live through the summer without your care. Consult a master gardener from the Cooperative Extension Service in your state, or perhaps someone you know who is a good gardener. Try to use compost instead of fertilizer, and avoid pesticides because of their effects on soil and children (see the Appendix, "Background to the Problem of Pesticides and Other Toxins"). Runoff from fertilizers and pesticides contributes to the formation of dead zones in bays and oceans like the Gulf of Mexico and the Chesapeake Bay.

* Set up a rain barrel, if space permits, to collect rainfall to use for watering plants. Also capture the water running out of downspouts and direct it to gardens. Help children become aware of the water cycle.

* Provide logs children can scramble over and balance on, boulders to climb on and jump from, and trees to climb, if possible. These items can supplement or replace commercial climbing equipment. Sometimes a play yard can be extended just to include a good climbing tree, which should be the right size for children's reach and abilities.

* Be mindful of universal design ideas to make the play area accessible and satisfying to all children (Goltsman 2011; Moore & Cosco 2007b; Natural Learning Initiative and the Center for Universal Design 2005; Ostroff 2011).

Because there are so many things to consider, consult experts whenever you can. A plan from a landscape architect gives direction to the project and keeps stakeholders moving together. A landscape architect also has knowledge and experience that program staff likely do not. Cooperative Extension staff, which may include master gardeners and the staffs of nature centers, the Department of Natural Resources, and parks and recreation departments, are usually eager to give time and advice.

Stories From the Field: Setting Boundaries

What is challenging about working with children outside is figuring out how to best bring our great indoor teaching with us when we go. When children go outside, whether it is into the woods or into a garden, they experience a sense of freedom and excitement. They have their own ways of relating to their surroundings that may or may not be compatible with our goals or expectations. Logistically, the open space can make setting limits difficult. I find it best to imagine outdoor spaces in much the same way that we do in our indoor classrooms.

First of all, we talk with the children and establish some non-negotiable guidelines, such as not harming any of the living things that we encounter. Perhaps we agree to leave what we find or harvest only with adult permission. We also create some boundaries in terms of where the children may explore and places that are off-limits. Establishing these guidelines beforehand is essential.

Next, I think of how I might help the children find a productive focus. Some children are able to gravitate to a kind of respectful exploration without any adult guidance. They may dig in a compost pile or collect fallen leaves. But, I need a back-up plan for children who have difficulty coming up with engaging and safe exploration. This might be a specific activity or curricular focus.

Whether the activity is structured or unstructured, the children will likely need some tools and materials such as magnifying glasses, cups, digging tools, clipboards, paper, pencils, or watercolor paint and paintbrushes. I need to think through in advance what these will be, how I will set them up, and how the kids will access them and put them away. The materials available will nourish and build depth into the activities. Just like in my indoor classroom, I need to teach the routines for taking care of these items and, most likely, I will teach this over time until the children have internalized the set-up, safety rules, and clean-up of each new material.

All of this may seem like a lot of trouble, but setting out with a large group of kids without the same kind of consideration that we use to set routines within our rooms is a recipe for frustration. If we utilize our skills in setting up our outdoor "classrooms," we are sure to find teaching outdoors fun, safe, and enriching. And we will want to do more of it!

—Abbe Futterman, co-founder and science teacher,
The Earth School & The Fifth Street Farm

Making over a play yard is challenging. Not everyone at a center or school will be eager to undertake the process, and some staff may be unsure of how to interact with children in a more nature-focused setting. They will need to understand that the environment itself teaches and facilitates children's interaction with it (see *Cultivating Outdoor Classrooms* by Eric Nelson, 2012, 39–51), and they will also need to know subject matter not yet part of most early childhood teacher education programs, such as the following (Nelson 2012):

- ✳ Fundamental understanding of plants and wild animals, growth and decay, natural cycles, and ecology
- ✳ Gardening skills
- ✳ Ability to help children explore and learn in a natural environment
- ✳ Skill in setting up activities in a natural environment
- ✳ Knowledge about cultivating, maintaining, and enhancing a natural environment (42)

Nelson (2012) outlines the process of developing outdoor spaces clearly. He includes advice about professional development for staff and how to develop the type of community that will provide children better resources and time and space for self-direction, discovery, and play. This may require a major shift in the way a program teaches. But as Erin Kenny of Cedarsong Nature School notes, eager, engaged children are the reward: "Children can't bounce off the walls if there are no walls."

Beyond Schools and School Yards

Dewey proposed that the whole surroundings of a school—the "wider country"—be used to educate. For many programs the wider country includes city streets, and many teachers, such as those at Bank Street in New York City, routinely lead city-based expeditions. However, expeditions to the "wider country" have been mostly curtailed. Field trips are often difficult to arrange; as Kirchen (2011) points out, they are "limited by logistics, expense, safety/liability, time constraints, weather conditions, lack of transportation, overcrowding, lack of volunteers/chaperones, or lack of accessibility for children with special needs" (24).

Ann Pelo (2009) defied this trend with repeated urban neighborhood explorations with preschoolers. She led the children to notice everything in their Seattle center's neighborhood: the sights, smells, sounds, rain, clouds, and changes. She wanted them to *know* their surroundings, and in knowing to become attached to them:

This is what I want for children: a sensual, emotional, and *conscious* connection to place, the sure, sweet knowledge of earth, air, sky. As a teacher, I want to foster in children an ecological identity, one that shapes them as surely as their cultural and social identities. I believe that this ecological identity, born in a particular place, opens children to a broader connection with the earth; love for a specific place makes possible love for other places. An ecological identity allows us to experience the earth as our home ground, and leaves us determined to live in honorable relationship with our planet. (30)

Pelo's belief in the power of knowing a place opens the possibility for teachers and children in all schools and centers to explore the environment around them. Clouds, birds, ants, broken concrete, rain running down streets—everything is worth observing and absorbing. The "wider country" is our home.

Curriculum for the Outdoors

Ann Pelo (2013) was watching toddler Dylan happily pitch pebbles into the lake when a loud shriek above alerted them to the singular presence of two bald eagles. Dylan briefly looked up and then returned to throwing pebbles. Ann realized that she was experiencing a "rare and holy thing to stand beneath twin eagles" (77). She debated pointing out the eagles' bright white heads, naming them, and introducing them, but Dylan was experiencing joy in throwing, the water, and stones. So Ann decided:

> "There would be no instruction to offer. What I can give Dylan, in this moment, is my reverence, my glad astonishment at our good fortune, my upward gaze and wordless watching" (77).

There are numerous resources for outdoor curriculum. Some schools and centers are bound to a prescribed curriculum and teach parts of it outdoors. Nature center preschools extend what is happening outdoors to indoor experiences. Two well-established environmental education programs, Project Learning Tree (2010) and Project WILD (2012), publish early childhood curriculum guides, and the North American Association for Environmental Education issues general guidelines for excellence in environmental education (2010). These guides are useful for teachers, but as David Sobel notes, prescribed curricula for outdoor experiences tend to limit the child —the whole point of exploring the outdoors is to discover for oneself what is in nature, mud and scrapes and all. Sobel (2012) believes that freely chosen experiences first create enthusiasm for nature, then lead to a love for living things, and finally nurture a sense of stewardship of the land. Banning and Sullivan (2011) offer sensitive examples of this type of curriculum in North

Carolina and elsewhere, and Pelo (2013) further describes her outdoor experiences with a Seattle toddler; Jan White's DVDs look at and interpret outdoors experiences with infants, toddlers, and 2-year-olds. White provides two especially valuable sources of curriculum ideas with her book *Playing and Learning Outdoors: Making Provision for High Quality Experiences in the Outdoor Environment With Children 3–7* (2014) and her blog http://janwhitenaturalplay.wordpress.com.

Outdoor Play Without Much Green

Urban schools are often constrained when it comes to providing outdoor play experiences. Three programs with limited space—Boston Public Schools, Scrapstore PlayPod, and Playworks—confronted this problem, and each arrived at a different solution. The Boston Schoolyard Initiative (BSI), an independent nonprofit organization, administers development and implementation grants to community groups. With strong support from longtime Mayor Thomas Menino, the BSI began in the early 1990s to transform asphalt-covered school yards into more appealing, natural play yards. More than 70 school yards, including one on a rooftop, now have gardens, rocks, logs, trees, and butterfly gardens on the edges, with play equipment and interesting graphics on the remaining asphalt (including, at one school, hopscotch in Chinese). Yards are distinctive, reflecting each community's needs and creativity. Funds came from the Boston Schoolyards Funders Collaborative, which collected them from numerous groups. In 2013, the BSI declared victory and closed. Now, however, the city of Oakland, California, is replicating this model in the Oakland School Initiative.

In the United Kingdom, the Scrapstore PlayPod program gathers clean, safe materials headed for landfills from community businesses, packs them into a Dumpster-size shed, parks it at the edge of a school yard, and opens the doors at lunchtime. An extended loose-parts playtime ensues, encouraging children to play creatively and reshaping recess to be fun, imaginative, and peaceful. Teachers and principals as well as children appreciate this program. More than 50 schools have adopted the PlayPod program (see www.playpods.co.uk). The following are videos of two programs using the PlayPod program: primary school children at www.youtube.com/watch?v=nqi1KyJJeKg and preschool children at www.playpods.co.uk/EarlyYears.aspx.

Teaching children games and helping them play successfully together is the solution to outdoor play, particularly recess time, offered by Playworks. The program operates in more than 380 schools in low-income communities in 23 cities around the country. Playworks provides a trained coach, often an AmeriCorps volunteer, who teaches children a raft of playful games, shows children how to resolve conflicts quickly so the play can keep going, works at recess and after school, and becomes a valued member of

the school community. In addition, teachers and principals receive training, and older students are trained to extend the playful, peaceful games approach to younger children. Research confirms that fighting and bullying occur less in schools using the Playworks program (Bleeker et al. 2012). See www.playworks.org.

What About Recess?

Recess as a time for children to play freely and actively has been slipping away for more than two decades. According to a 2010 study from the Centers for Disease Control and Prevention (CDC), only 20 states require recess in elementary schools. Since recess is the prime time for outdoor play in most K–12 schools, it appears that outdoor time is not highly valued. Physical education is required by 37 states, some of which allow recess time to meet the requirement. For licensed, regulated child care centers, the CDC reported that only eight states require children to engage in "moderate- or vigorous-intensity physical activity" (10). It is a very good thing to provide play yards rich in opportunities for exploring nature and other activities, but to what end if children have little time to spend in them?

In response to findings that time for physical activity in many schools is lacking, the American Academy of Pediatrics (AAP; 2013a) issued a strong call for recess, focusing on the health of today's underexercised and overweight youngsters. The report, "The Crucial Role of Recess in School," is available at http://pediatrics.aappublications.org/content/131/1/183.full. The National Association for Sport and Physical Education (NASPE 2006) has a position statement, "Recess for Elementary School Students," that is useful for teachers who want to restore or revitalize recess in their programs. It is found at www.aahperd.org/naspe/standards/upload/recess-for-elementary-school-students-2006.pdf.

In a comprehensive review of research on recess (2013), noted scholar and advocate Olga Jarrett concluded that recess supports the development of social skills, self-control, emotional health, and physical strength and skills. Such research can help turn the anti-recess tide, but teachers and parents may have to convince administrators and policy makers that both rich outdoor play spaces and the time to explore them are necessary for children to thrive. Happily, some school systems seem to be reversing the trend toward less time for recess. Chicago Public Schools, for example, banned recess for 30 years but is now restoring it.

We have every indication that playing outdoors, particularly in nature-rich environments, benefits children enormously. Why then is outdoor play an issue for administrators, teachers, and families? Possibly our enthusiasm is muted by aspects of outdoor play that trouble us, which are explored in the next chapter.

Reflections

* I wonder how I would go about making our yard like some of those described.

* What resistance would I encounter?

* Who might I enlist as allies?

What You Can Do

1. Dig a hole in the corner of the yard, supply some shovels, and see what happens.

2. Adopt a stick policy and enjoy the creativity as well as care for this "new" equipment.

3. Encourage collection of natural treasures such as rocks, pebbles, leaves, pinecones, and more.

4. Ask your park district for some lengths (two to three feet long) of fallen trees. Make a circle of stumps and establish a log place where children can carry and roll logs around,

5. Whatever curriculum plans you have for the indoors, adapt them for the outdoors.

6. Read Jan White's blog (janwhitenaturalplay.wordpress.com) for joyful inspiration.

7. If there is room in your yard, ask the manager of a construction site to find you a good boulder or two—ones that children can climb on, jump off, and make things on. Ask the manager to place the boulder or boulders securely in the yard. Construction people have equipment and experience to do this quickly, safely, and enthusiastically.

Precautions
Outdoors

Several years ago, as director of a large suburban child care center with generous, well-used outdoor spaces, I tried to require my staff to use sunscreen themselves during the program day. Since modeling healthy behaviors for children was part of our curriculum, I wanted the children to see the staff applying their own sunscreen. I also felt concerned about the amount of time the staff spent outdoors without protection from harmful sun rays. But the staff rebelled against being *required* to use sunscreen—I had crossed a line with them.

I did, however, purchase sunscreen for each class and keep the supplies replenished. This worked! Staff increased their use of sunscreen. My next strategy was to require their attendance at a professional training course on sun safety. The entire staff completed the course, and I noticed a definite uptick in sunscreen usage afterward.

Over time, though, usage seemed to slip. So I wonder: How can we keep a good practice going?

My state considers sunscreen a medicine that requires parental permission to apply to children's skin. Teachers find applying it to children something of a nuisance, so they encourage parents to apply it at home. Skin cancer is a major public health problem. Between the parents who don't put sunscreen on their children, and the teachers who don't do it, I worry about the children's safety. What's the solution here?

—Nancy Jean Wagner

Nancy encouraged her teachers to take precautions for their own safety. She was aware of the tension between families and teachers in her program regarding whose responsibility it is to ensure that children use sunscreen sufficiently—the families may apply sunscreen in the morning before the children go to child care, but there is a whole day of potential reapplications to consider. Also involved in this is the question of "which sunscreen?" Which sunscreen is most effective, which is least likely to cause allergies, and which has the least harmful chemicals?

Answering these questions and others related to children being safe outdoors is the focus of this chapter. Underlying the information presented is what is now called the "precautionary principle" (see sidebar for definition), a legal standard in many other developed countries but not yet in the United States. This principle states that if evidence exists that an action or a substance may be harmful to humans and the environment, precautionary measures should be taken even before complete scientific data exists. This common sense principle is one that people who care for children follow instinctively.

The precautionary principle is important as we consider not only sunscreen but also insect and tick repellents, pesticides, sandbox sand, soil in the play yard, and artificial turf, because the regulatory system in the United States does not follow the precautionary principle by law. The United States instead uses the principle of "risk assessment," which means scientific studies are conducted to ascertain how much risk is involved. Such studies are not conducted on small children because the controlled, randomized methods makes them unethical for children. Fortunately, some non-governmental groups have attempted to establish safety standards, so there is current information, much of which is presented in this chapter.

The Wingspread Consensus Statement on the Precautionary Principle

In January 1998 a diverse group of scientists, environmental activists, and others issued a statement relating to public health and environmental decisions:

> When an activity raises threats of harm to human health or the environment, precautionary measures should be taken even if some cause and effect relationships are not fully established scientifically. In this context the proponent of an activity, rather than the public, should bear the burden of proof. The process of applying the precautionary principle must be open, informed, and democratic and must include potentially affected parties. It must also involve an examination of the full range of alternatives, including no action. (Science and Environmental Health Network 2013)

To keep children's outdoor experiences beneficial and positive, teachers need to take a variety of safety precautions. Being outdoors is a natural condition. However, being sheltered from the elements and hazards is also natural, or the species would not have survived. This chapter offers information on minimizing children's exposure to harmful sunrays, toxicants, and other dangers.

Sun Exposure

Although the sun is the source of life and energy on Earth, its ultraviolet radiation (UVR) is harmful to people. Skin cancer is the most common type of cancer, affecting one in five Americans. It is considered a major public health problem (Balk 2011).

Short-term damage from the sun can cause sunburn; long-term damage can include cancer, cataracts, and possibly macular degeneration. Two specific phenomena contribute to overexposure to the sun: the thinned ozone layer surrounding the Earth, which allows more UVR to reach the earth than previously, and the Western fashion of "being tan." Furthermore, according to the American Academy of Pediatrics (AAP), "Public awareness of the risk is not optimal, overall compliance with sun protection is inconsistent, and melanoma rates continue to rise" (Balk 2011, 791).

How to Limit Sun Damage

In surveys conducted in 2000, 2005, and 2010 (Centers for Disease Control and Prevention [CDC] 2012c), fewer than half of young adults reported using sun protective measures. One blistering sunburn in childhood or adolescence more than doubles a person's chance of developing melanoma later in life, according to the Skin Cancer Foundation (2014). Early childhood professionals can do five things to help protect children:

1. Model routine use of effective sunscreen with low toxicity.

2. Provide shady outdoor places to play.

3. Provide or ask families to provide hats and clothes that shade children's bodies.

4. Have children wear sunglasses that filter out radiation.

5. Teach children, families, and staff about sun protection.

Routine use of sunscreen. Many early childhood teachers administer sunscreen that offers the valuable but sometimes incomplete protection from UVR. There are two kinds of UVR: UVB rays, which cause sunburn, and UVA rays, which penetrate deeper into the skin. The Environmental Working Group publishes an annual safety and efficacy ratings of hundreds of sunscreens (see www.ewg.org for the latest guide). It is important to check labels. Early childhood settings may want to make information about recommended sunscreen products available to parents. The Campaign for Safe Cosmetics (www.safecosmetics.org) also advocates for safe and healthy sunscreen. Teachers and families should be aware that 5- to 12-year-old children in one study did not apply enough sunscreen to provide the SPF (sun protection factor) recorded on the product's label, although they did apply more from a pump applicator than either a roll-on or squeeze bottle (Diaz et al. 2012). If children apply their own sunscreen, they should be taught the correct amount and procedure.

Shady places to play. Shade in the outdoor play area provides additional protection for children's skin. Play areas should have some shade throughout the day. To learn about designing shade structures, see the CDC's "Shade Planning for America's Schools" (www.cdc.gov/cancer/skin/pdf/shade_planning.pdf). In addition to information on shade structures, this website includes advice on plantings for shade that also provide beauty and habitats for animals, and on organizing the school community to create shady places in the play yard.

Sun protection from hats and clothing. Australia has the world's highest incidence of skin cancer, which has led that country to focus

Guidelines on Using Sunscreen in Centers and Schools

- Develop a policy about whether sunscreen is supplied by program staff or by families.

- Provide a release form to families that explains how your program uses sunscreen and requests information about potential allergies to it. Get written permission from families to apply sunscreen to their child.

- Select broad-spectrum sunscreen (protects against UVA and UVB rays) with a factor of SPF 30, or ask families to provide it.

- Apply sunscreen to all exposed areas of skin, including cheeks, neck, arms, legs, behind the ears, and on the nose.

- Apply sunscreen 15 to 30 minutes before children go out, even on cloudy days. Reapply sunscreen every two hours. Remember to reapply after swimming or running through a sprinkler. (Mankiw 2011, 23)

on sun protection (Australian Institute of Health and Welfare & Australasian Association of Cancer Registries 2012). Children often wear broad-brimmed hats and long-sleeved shirts and long pants outdoors. Because recess time in the primary grades in the United States is typically during the peak time for sun exposure (10 a.m.–4 p.m.), some schools have held fundraisers to buy broad-brimmed hats for all the children. See the sidebar "Sun Protection From Clothing" for more tips.

Sunglasses. All children older than 6 months should wear shatter-resistant sunglasses. Sunglasses should wrap around the eyes and block 97–100 percent of both UVA and UVB rays (AAP 2012c). According to the Skin Cancer Foundation,

> Children under age 10 are at a high risk for skin and eye damage from UVR. The skin on their eyelids and around their eyes is more delicate and vulnerable than adult skin. "And until about age 10, the lens of a child's eye is clear, allowing greater solar penetration and thus greater UVR-induced ocular changes," explains Adelaide A. Hebert, MD, professor and vice chair of dermatology, University of Houston. "After that, the lens starts to become more opaque, providing better protection." (2012)

Just as with sunscreen, reading labels on sunglasses is key.

Heavy cloud cover filters some UVR from reaching Earth but not all. To learn the amount of UVR predicted for a particular place on the following day, consult the Environmental Protection Agency's (EPA) UV Index at http://www2.epa.gov/sunwise/uv-index. This is useful information when planning outdoor activities.

Educating children, families, and staff. In an effort to minimize sun damage to children, the EPA offers the Sunwise Program for educators. To receive a free toolkit of curriculum materials, register for the program at www.epa.gov/sunwise/becoming.html. An online video provides more background and an overview of the activities in the curriculum (www.epa.gov/sunwise/tools.html). Dartmouth Medical School provides a curriculum that begins with activities for young children in centers (http://sunsafe.dartmouth.edu).

As you implement the five actions on page 46 to help limit sun damage to children's skin, keep in mind that children do need some direct sunlight for their bodies to produce the vitamin D necessary for good health, especially of bones. While the amount of vitamin D needed is the subject of considerable research (Office of Dietary Supplements 2011), supplementa-

---

Sun Protection From Clothing

- Encourage families to dress children in lightweight clothing that covers their bodies as much as possible. This offers additional protection against the sun's rays. Some clothing has sun protection embedded in the fabric.

- Request that families send in hats with a broad brim, labeled with their child's name.

- Advise families to send in sunglasses with labels stating that they provide 100-percent UV protection. The best way to protect eyes is to wear sunglasses, but not all sunglasses are the same. (Mankiw 2011, 23)

tion is recommended by the AAP (2012a), which recently stated that 4 of 10 toddlers and children are deficient in this vitamin. Does sunlight coming through the window count as direct exposure? Ordinary glass blocks UVB but not UVA. Different regions of the world experience differing strengths of sunlight; consult your local health authorities for the amount of sun time and vitamin D needed.

Early childhood centers might provide a summary handout to families explaining the five-action sun protection described in this section. The CDC provides a downloadable color brochure at www.cdc.gov/cancer/skin/pdf/CYC-ParentsBrochure.pdf.

Regulatory Changes

Most states have laws or regulations that limit schools in their efforts to protect children from UVR. For example, many states consider sunscreen a medicine and regulate its use during school. Some schools forbid children to wear hats. School sites set their own policies about the use of these and other sun-protective articles. The California Education Code Section 35183.5 requires that

> Each schoolsite shall allow for outdoor use during the schoolday, articles of sun-protective clothing that pupils would be allowed to wear outdoors, including, but not limited to, hats. . . . Each schoolsite shall allow pupils the use of sunscreen during the schoolday without a physician's note or prescription. (State of California 2002)

Provisions for shady yards, sunglasses, lip balm, and education for all school staff are not in California's code at present but are suggested by the Sun Safety for Kids organization, which pushed for the new regulations. Teachers concerned about restrictive center and school policies on sun protection might consult this organization for suggestions on achieving change (go to www.sunsafetyforkids.org).

Sand, Soil, and Artificial Turf

Children spend more time on the ground than adults and are exposed to more of what is on the ground through their skin, mouths, and noses. Awareness of what is in the natural soil or sand, or of late, artificial turf, is important.

Sandbox Sand

Although sandbox sand is not commonly considered a toxic substance, sand manufactured from ground quartz contains crystalline silica dust, which is carcinogenic and primarily affects the lungs. When buying sand, centers and schools should read the Materials Safety Data Sheet (MSDS) for the product. Because sand might contain "toxic or harmful ingredients such as tremolite, an asbestos-like substance," *Caring for Our Children: National Health and Safety Performance Standards; Guidelines for Early Care and Education Programs* recommends using sand that is "free of organic, toxic, or harmful materials" (American Academy of Pediatrics, American Public Health Association, & National Resource Center for Health and Safety in Child Care and Early Education 2011, 274). Look for sand, such as natural river or beach sand (AAP 2013b), or Santastik Play Sand, that does not contain tremolite or crushed crystalline silica (quartz).

Gardens and Digging Areas

If you are planning a garden or designating an area for dirt play and digging, first test the soil for lead toxicity. The Cooperative Extension System of the US Department of Agriculture (USDA) can facilitate the testing. Contact the local agent through the Cooperative Extension System website at www.csrees. usda.gov/Extension/. If the soil has a toxic level of lead, arrange for new soil to be brought in for

digging and gardening. If children will not be handling the soil, minimize the risk of contamination by raising the pH of the soil to make the lead less available to the plants, by adding organic matter to bind the lead, or by covering the soil with sod (Rosen 2010). Locate gardens and digging areas away from old buildings and roadways, where lead may be deposited. As a precaution, have children wash their hands after playing outdoors.

Artificial Turf

Synthetic turf, which uses lead chromate to improve the colorfastness of the grass blades, increased in popularity over the last decade. In 2008 the Consumer Product Safety Commission (CPSC) tested various artificial turfs and concluded that while samples of older turf contained more lead than samples of newer turf, none of them was likely to endanger children. However, the turf industry adopted tougher standards to virtually eliminate lead in all its pigments by January 2012 (Synthetic Turf Council 2008). Teachers, administrators, and families who wish to have turf tested free of charge can send a small sample to the Center for Environmental Health per the instructions at www.ceh.org/lead-in-artificial-turf/. Other concerns about artificial turf include the following:

* In the sun it becomes hotter than natural grass, which may create an uncomfortable outdoor environment for young children.

* It is made of used ground-up tires, which contain numerous toxicants.

* It is hard to keep clean.

* Installation and upkeep are more expensive than grass.

Pesticides and Integrated Pest Management (IPM)

Whenever possible, programs and schools should avoid the use of pesticides—that is, insecticides, rodenticides, fungicides, and herbicides. The practice of Integrated Pest Management (IPM), which minimizes the use of pesticides, is required or recommended in 25 states as of 2013. (Visit Beyond Pesticides for more information on IPM at www.beyondpesticides.org/infos-ervices/pcos/IPM.php.)

Indoors, IPM practices control pests with non-chemical methods—strenuously avoiding pesticides with carcinogens, endocrine disruptors, nervous or immune system interrupters, or reproductive or developmental toxicants—and use only "least toxic" chemicals as a last resort. Outdoors, IPM adheres to these guidelines and favors organic management of grounds, school gardens, and playing fields, minimizing the use of chemical fertilizers.

* Wood preserved with chemicals should not be used to build garden beds or play equipment; the carcinogenic wood preservative CCA (chromated copper arsenate) has been banned for nearly a decade for home use but is still on some public play equipment. CCA turns wood dark and has a characteristic aroma. Try to avoid using it, and wash hands after touching it. If the wood is important to your playground and you want to save it, it needs to be sealed at least once a year.

✳ If you use mulch, try to determine its origins—did it come from an organic producer, or will the mulch introduce pesticide residues into the play space? Teachers in agricultural areas need to be aware of pesticide drift, which occurs when aerial spraying of crop fields in windy conditions causes pesticides to enter school air space.

For a more detailed discussion of IPM and to find out whether your state requires its use, visit www.beyondpesticides.org. Beyond Pesticides also offers free subscriptions to *The School Pesticide Monitor,* published six times yearly. Beyond Pesticides offers opportunities to become involved in efforts to seek change, with petitions to sign and suggestions for contacting legislators and policy makers. A parent information sheet is also available on the website.

The Pesticide Action Network North America (PANNA) also offers activist possibilities and a thorough, searchable database of various chemicals (www.pesticideinfo.org). This database is helpful for investigating the safety of a product.

Insect and Tick Repellent

Biting and stinging creatures can be a concern in the outdoors. While most bites are simply bothersome, others can trigger a serious allergic response or transmit disease. Mosquitoes may carry West Nile virus. Ticks may carry Lyme disease or Rocky Mountain spotted fever. The National Pesticide Information Center (www.npic.orst.edu/) has abundant information on pests and pesticides, including links to maps of where pest-related diseases have been reported. The US Geological Survey (USGS) has maps that show similar information (http://diseasemaps.usgs.gov/index.html).

Unfortunately, the most effective chemical for repelling insects, DEET, can adversely affect the nervous system. DEET is found in most insect repellents, typically at 10–30 percent concentrations. According to the AAP (2012b), repellents containing up to 30 percent DEET concentrations may be used on children; however, it does not recommend using insect repellent on children younger than 2 months. Another common ingredient in tick repellent, permethrin, also affects the nervous system and is a possible carcinogen. Considering the delicate skin of young children and their developing nervous systems, teachers subscribing to the precautionary principle may want to avoid using products with DEET and permethrin. Beyond Pesticides provides information on other, less harmful chemicals in its document "How to Repel Mosquitoes Safely" (see www.beyondpesticides.org/mosquito/documents/LesstoxRepellents.pdf).

You can discourage the presence of mosquitoes by eliminating standing water in outdoor areas, in which they breed, or by adding fish if a pond is part of your outdoor space (fish eat mosquito eggs and larvae), or by using mosquito netting around outdoor structures where children play. Another strategy is to turn on a fan in the play area; mosquitoes are weak fliers and cannot approach people as easily in a breeze.

Lead

Lead has been mined for thousands of years. In the United States it was added to paint until banned in 1978 and to gasoline until it was banned in 1996. Piston engine airplanes still use leaded gas, a concern for children living or attending school near an airport where these small planes land and take off (EPA 2010). Since lead does not break down, it lingers on the sides of roads and highways and around the edges of houses and buildings built and painted before 1978. Young children sometimes like to lick lead paint surfaces, such as windowsills, or eat the paint chips because of their sweet taste. Old, poorly maintained buildings are thus a hazard to young children. Older cities typically have dangerous levels of lead in their soil from both buildings and manufacturing processes.

The banning of lead from most gasoline sharply decreased the number of children poisoned by lead. In addition, following the 2011 release of a major study by the National Toxicology Program, and a report from its advisory committee (CDC 2012b), in May 2012 the CDC lowered the blood lead level at which public health actions should be initiated, from 10 micrograms of lead per deciliter of blood to 5 micrograms (CDC 2012a). The 2012 CDC report stated that the level should be zero, as lead is never safe for children. About 450,000 children ages 1–5 are now eligible for monitoring and other public health action (CDC 2012b).

High blood lead levels in children are associated with decreased fetal growth, lower birth weight, decreased cognitive functioning and academic achievement, and increased neurobehavioral problems, such as attention-deficit/hyperactivity disorder (ADHD). The CDC 2012 report's main emphasis is on prevention and has implications for the type of housing children live in:

Primary prevention is a strategy that emphasizes the prevention of lead exposure, rather than a response to exposure after it has taken place. Primary prevention is necessary because the effects of lead appear to be irreversible. In the US, this strategy will largely require that children not live in older housing with lead-based paint hazards. Screening children for elevated BLLs [blood lead levels] and dealing with their housing only when their BLL is already elevated should no longer be acceptable practice. (CDC 2012b, ix)

This recommendation might have implications for substandard housing in which more than two million children live (Coley et al. 2013).

Lead poisoning is a familiar public health topic, so there are many resources for teachers and families. See, for example, "Frequently Asked Questions About Lead" on the EPA website (www.epa.gov/reg3wcmd/lp-faqhealth.htm) or consult the National Lead Information Center [NLIC]; www2.epa.gov/lead/forms/lead-hotline-national-lead-information-center) or your state lead program.

Because it is an element, lead does not break down into anything else. It remains—in soil, in paint, in bodies. It is not readily taken up by plants, so it remains in the soil. We must take abundant precautions to prevent it from entering human bodies, where it creates damage. Teachers need to be aware of how children in their programs may be affected, and to help families and their health providers to prevent and, as much as possible, remediate the effects of lead poisoning.

Environmental Injustices

Since the late 1980s, a disproportionate number of toxic waste sites have been located in minority communities (Bullard et al. 2007). Polluting facilities—smelters, refineries, and waste and chemical plants—are often clustered in a community (Cowell 2012). A disproportionate number are also located in the South and in rural communities (for example, many mountaintop removal mines in West Virginia affect white families in communities with low income). Robert Bullard, a leading environmental justice scholar and activist, notes that environmental justice is about both people and the natural environment. He observes,

> **Toxic Load, or Chemical Body Burden**
>
> Toxic load, or chemical body burden, refers to the accumulated amount of toxins, both naturally occurring and manufactured, that are present in a human body at a point in time. These toxins may result from environmental exposure or chemical ingestion.

Too many Americans don't have a clue about what happens outside their own neighborhood. They assume that everybody shares equally the effects of pollution or degradation, but that's not true. Our society is still very segregated along class and race lines, and the poor and minorities suffer more adverse effects. (Cowell 2012, 6)

Just as a person has a toxic load, or chemical body burden, so each community has a toxic load. Bullard states,

If you live in a community of color, you are two and a half times more likely to live near a polluting facility. That's part of the reason why ZIP codes and neighborhoods are consistent, powerful predictors of people's health. (Cowell 2012, 7)

The United States is slowly grappling with this problem. Each federal government agency, for example, is under an executive order to "make achieving environmental justice part of its mission" (Office of Environmental Justice 2011, 1). The EPA's environmental justice webpages present additional information on the effort along with short first-person videos that bring to life cases of environmental injustice (www. epa.gov/environmentaljustice/). A Native American from the Southwest points out that *cultures* are afflicted by environmental injustice along with *people*—in particular cultures that consider all living components interconnected (see the sidebar). As educators, we need to be aware that many children and their families endure a heavy chemical burden and cultural disconnect as a result of toxins and toxicants in the environment.

Industrial pollution affects all neighborhoods and people to some degree—the parts are not separated from the whole. If your work is in a place with a heavy toxic burden, it will have an impact on your work.

The Seriousness of the Toxic Burden

A number of sources (e.g., Landrigan, Lambertini, & Birnbaum 2012; Shabecoff & Shabecoff 2008) assert that toxins and toxicants from a variety of sources have a poisonous effect on our bodies. The Environmental Working Groups (2009) tested the umbilical cord blood of 10 infants in 2005 and 10 more in 2009, finding up to 287 chemicals in the infants' cord blood. This study indicates that children are exposed to harmful substances even before they are born. The CDC (2013) published four national biomonitoring studies involving children and adults, most recently in 2009 with updates in 2013. These reports assess the exposure of the US population to toxic substances and environmental chemicals (see www.cdc.gov/biomonitoring).

Many scientists, policy makers, and citizens in the United States have called for adherence to "the precautionary principle." This common sense principle is an excellent guide to use to protect children from exposure to toxic substances.

Reflections

∗ Seeing the wide range of issues regarding children's safety outdoors, how do I use this knowledge to fuel activism?

∗ Where do I find allies to share and address my concerns?

What You Can Do

1. As early childhood professionals, our first duty is to keep children safe. We need to inform ourselves and the children's families about the need for and importance of clean water, air, and soil. The Children's Environmental Health Network is one source of current environment information (www.cehn.org).

2. Use information or activities from Dartmouth's Sun Safe program (http://cancer.dartmouth.edu/melanoma_skin/sunsafe_early_years.html) to raise awareness about sun safety at the early childhood setting where you work.

3. Learn about individual opportunities for advocacy for safe and healthy sunscreen at the Campaign for Safe Cosmetics (www.safecosmetics.org).

3. If IPM is not used in your school or center, provide your administrator or director with information about its use.

4. If the information in this chapter alerts you to problems with your outdoor space, try to find a way to make changes.

Children's Spiritual Development and Nature

Deborah Schein

I once worked at a child development center where the children had to walk down a narrow hallway several times a day to use the restrooms. The hallway had high windows facing west. The children could not see out the windows, but still something wondrous emerged. On sunny days, we could see our shadows. On cloudy days, no shadows appeared.

When shadows did appear, the children began to create shadow games: touching shadow to shadow, covering up parts of their bodies and those of others, noticing the size and direction of shadows, and delighting in how the plants hanging in the high windows also produced shadows on the wall, the floor, and the children themselves. In fact, the windows also produced shadows.

With a simple reminder from me to the children to take note of the shadows, the walk down the hall took on new meaning as the light and shadows created moments of joy and wonder for the children. Even the cloudy days stimulated big questions that reflected the children's wonder: "Where are our shadows?," "Where is the sun?," and "What's going on?"

Later in the afternoon, after naptime, the children and I would revisit the power of light with a few strategically placed prisms in the west-facing classroom windows. The children grew to expect rainbows on sunny days. When a rainbow occurred, everyone felt happy. On cloudy days, we learned not to be sad, as we all understood that the sun would eventually reappear on another day.

In this way, nature exploration with light provided daily spiritual moments filled with shadows, rainbows, questions, joy, awe, and wonderment for the children. Nature and spiritual development together make a strong pedagogical tool for all styles of learners.

Despite the hazards described in Chapter 3, researchers and early childhood educators describe nature as important for human development (Kellert 2005; Louv 2008; Bailie 2012). Kellert shares that nothing less than the future of our species is at stake in maintaining and restoring a relationship between human development and nature (2012). This same attitude is reflected in the growing number of forest and nature schools, which provide children with natural playspaces (Armitage 2009; Anggard 2010; Bailie 2012; O'Brien & Murray 2006).

Spending time in nature is often tied to spiritual development (Bailie 2012; Baumgartner & Buchanan 2010; Kellert 2005; Louv 2008). Louv (2008) writes "that all spiritual life begins with a sense of wonder, and that one of the first windows to wonder is the natural world" (356).

According to Baumgartner and Buchanan (2010) "[i]n using developmentally appropriate practices, teachers should intentionally address all aspects of a child's being, the spiritual along with the physical and the cognitive" (90). These practices focus on meeting children where they are, seeing children as unique individuals, and being responsive to the social and cultural contexts in which they live (Copple & Bredekamp 2009).

> **Spiritual moments:**
> Feeling wonder, awe, joy, and inner peace

According to Roehlkepartain and colleagues (2006) and Schein (2012), very little research has been found that focuses on young children's spiritual development. This chapter shares the findings of a research study on spiritual development of young children living within the United States. One goal was to begin to define spiritual development so that it might be incorporated into early childhood education and developmentally appropriate practices. The results of the study highlight the existence of a system of spiritual development. In this study, a system is defined as parts of subsystems collected and used for a common goal (McNamara 2007).

This system begins with love and attachment (Carlson 2006; Gopnik, Meltzoff, & Kuhl 2001; Honig 2002; NAEYC 2008; Siegel & Hartzell 2003), deep connections (Schein 2012), and a sense of belonging (Baumgartner & Buchanan 2010) that work together to ignite a young child's absorbent mind (Montessori 1967) and the development of self-awareness and personal identity (Schein 2012). This system also calls for educators to provide environments where each child's disposition is matched to spiritual moments capable of filling the child's inner self with wonder, awe, joy, and inner peace (Schein 2012). These moments will be discussed later in this chapter. The third part of this system shows complex dispositions where children respond to their world with caring, kindness, empathy, and reverence (Schein 2012).

Disposition implies a child's nature, character, and temperament (Katz & Katz 2009).

This chapter will describe how this system works and how it relies upon children spending time *with* nature (up close so nature can be touched and examined) and *in* nature (outdoors so that children are part of nature). Other studies will be discussed that that either directly or indirectly connect nature experiences with spiritual development.

Exploring Theories Behind the Connection Between Spiritual Development and Nature

The connection between nature and spiritual development has a substantial theoretical basis. Many theorists have seen the value in and importance of studying the spiritual development of young children. Etzioni (2001), Fowler (1995), Gardner (1999), and Montessori (1963), for example, all write about the power of human spirituality, its presence at birth, and the positive role it plays in developing a whole, well-balanced individual. Using terms such as *empathy, caring, kindness,* and *wonderment,* Etzioni as well as Gardner, Csikszentmihalyi, and Damon (2001) imply that nurturing children's spirituality can lead to the creation of a better society. Following is a brief discussion of some theorists' contribution to our understanding of how children's spirituality is fostered by their nature experiences.

Montessori

Montessori (1963) speaks of the *horme,* or vital force, that guides each child toward growth, independence, and a desire to learn. Children's spiritual development is stimulated first by loving relationships and then through exploration of real, natural, and beautiful things. Although spiritual development relies upon relationships, it differs from social and emotional development in that spiritual development takes place deeply, internally, and is extremely personal. It is about a person's capacity to radiate sparks of spiritualness from within (Fowler 1995; Montessori 1963). Spirituality is not physical; it cannot be touched, and yet it fills up a person. This language, when connected to Montessori's idea of vital force, allows for a new way of talking about human growth and development.

Buber

Buber (1923 [1996]) describes three "spheres within which the world of relationships arises—life with nature, life with other persons, and life with spiritual beings" (57). He addresses the spiritual interchange between infants'

predispositions to seek out something larger than themselves and their relationships with individuals, groups, and the environment: Attachment and love lead infants to seek out familiar, friendly, or loving faces; an interesting toy; or varied textures, sounds, or tastes. Increased focus and intensity emerge as infants explore these relationships. This process continues throughout childhood as children build relationships with people and things they see, touch, smell, hear, and taste. When children explore nature at a young age and when they are encouraged to use all of their senses in this exploration, nature becomes a significant part of their existence.

Reggio Emilia

The Reggio Emilia approach extends Montessori's and Buber's theories by adding an understanding of children's needs and desires for socially constructing knowledge through language, big questions, and small-group investigations that often emerge directly from children's exploration in nature. Shadow, light, color, and water exploration are examples of investigatory play that delights and nurtures children's spiritual development as they build personal and collective relationships with the world around them.

Reggio Emilia educators often use the metaphor of the hundred languages of children to describe how children learn from a myriad of artistic expressions as each experience is capable of "bringing a new language for dialogue" (Gandini et al. 2005, 169). Language is believed to communicate thought (Vygotsky 1962), thereby children's exposure to a hundred languages provides children with a variety of ways to communicate, to reflect, and to know the world and themselves.

Gardner

In his initial theory of multiple intelligences, Gardner described seven intelligences: linguistic, logical–mathematical, musical, spatial, bodily-kinesthetic, interpersonal, and intrapersonal (Gardner 1993). Later he encompassed spiritual development with the additions of the naturalistic and existential intelligences. Naturalistic intelligence easily meets all of Gardner's criteria for becoming an intelligence and offers a popular and important perspective for the development of a child's spirituality; however, existential intelligence receives only a partial acknowledgment (Gardner 1999) because it is heavily influenced by cultural values (Gardner 1993).

Elements of Spirituality

Baumgartner and Buchanan (2010) identify three common elements of spirituality: "a sense of belonging, a respect for self and others, and an awareness and appreciation of the unknown" (91).

* **A sense of belonging.** Young children belong to various social networks—their families, their class, their community, and the world. Their connections to these social networks are strengthened when they do something, such as performing a classroom or household chore or comforting someone with a hug, that benefits the people around them.

* **A respect for self and others.** Teachers address spirituality when they show respect to children and encourage children to respect each other. Acknowledging children's strong emotions, modeling how to solve problems, and supporting creativity (such as through open-ended art experiences) are a few ways to model and teach children respect for self and others.

✳ **An awareness and appreciation of the unknown.** Curiosity, a sense of wonder, and time to enjoy the outside world are important aspects of spirituality.

Theorists and researchers have therefore seen nurturing a child's spirituality as supporting the development of a child's sense of self and the development of positive relationships that lead children to explore their surroundings. Knowledgeable, supportive, and responsive teachers can create an optimal environment for exploration. Such environments offer appropriate and interesting stimuli and challenges, literacy-rich activities, periods of uninterrupted play, and opportunities for nature exploration (Blain & Eady 2002; Kellert 2005). That children are wired to learn is now a known and accepted understanding (Goleman 1995; Lally, Mangione, & Greenwald 2006; Shonkoff & Phillips 2000). Through exploration and a variety of experiences a child's "brain and the biological pathways" are set to influence "intelligence, literacy, behavior, and physical and mental health" (Mustard 2005, 15; see also NAEYC 2008; National Scientific Council on the Developing Child 2007; Siegel & Hartzell 2003; Vandell 2004). Exploration and experiences also influence the spiritual side of human development (Harris 2007; Kirmani & Kirmani 2009; Surr 2011; Wilson 2012a).

The process of acquiring thought and language accentuates children's development in the cognitive, social, emotional, and spiritual domains. Language helps children express their thoughts and feelings about what they are experiencing—the meaning their intrapersonal and interpersonal experiences hold for them (Gardner 1999) and the awe, wonderment, and sense of self they are developing. Language also helps children understand and connect with all that is outside of themselves, and their understandings become internalized (Vygotsky 1962). From this awareness, children expand their sense of self, developing a will, motivation, ethical understanding, and a sense of responsibility (Kagan 2004; Montessori 1967; Mustakova-Possardt 2004).

The relationship between spiritual development and nature is complicated and intricate. The following discussion explores this complex connection and outlines a model for spiritual development.

Understanding Spiritual Development

While digging for worms with a group of young children on a playground at an urban early childhood center, I marveled that the children were excited, charmed, and calmed all at the same time. I wondered what was so remarkable about simple worms that they could produce this effect.

When I began looking for answers to this question and others about children's spiritual development, I discovered myriad materials on spiritual thought. Very few, however, were peer-reviewed articles, and only a handful discussed spirituality as an innate disposition. The literature revealed no shared definition and no unified theory on the spiritual development of young children living in the United States. Leading American early childhood curricula and other influential resources, such as *Developmentally Appropriate Practice in Early Childhood Programs Serving Children From Birth Through Age 8* from NAEYC (Copple & Bredekamp 2009), do not mention children's spiritual development. Researchers document an absence of a theoretical base, which has limited research efforts in spiritual development (Giesenberg 2007; Harris 2007; Kirmani & Kirmani 2009; Surr 2011). So I designed a study to provide a starting point for future research and discussion in the early childhood community (Schein 2012).

> Spiritual development is stimulated first by loving relationships and then through exploration of real, natural, and beautiful things. It relies upon relationships and takes place deeply and internally. It is extremely personal.

The study engaged 12 experienced early childhood educators in extensive interviews and conversations. These participants were (1) skilled observers of young children from infancy through age 7; (2) interested in the process of spiritual development; (3) able to distinguish between spirituality and religion while acknowledging the overlap between them; and (4) interested in early childhood practices that might foster spiritual development.

I asked the participants the following research questions:

1. What is the nature of spiritual development of young children? How might it be defined with regard to young children, beginning at birth?

2. What kinds of learning activities and experiences foster a child's spiritual development?

3. Has spiritual development been outwardly addressed? If so, how, and why?

4. What factors inhibit a child's spiritual development?

A Model for Spiritual Development

Using the educators' responses to these questions, I constructed a two-phase model for understanding how spiritual development occurs in young children. In this model, spiritual development is viewed as cyclical; once ignited by spiritual moments, children's connections and dispositions continue to strengthen each other.

> Deep connections begin when children seek connections with others, with nature, and with big questions that are capable of taking children beyond themselves.

The first phase consists of (1) the process by which children begin their spiritual journeys (2) the manner in which their dispositions and the deep connections they make through their relationships continue to work together throughout their lives and (3) how complex dispositions generate more and better relationships (see the figure "Phase 1: Deep Connections and Deep Dispositions").

The second phase includes the types of moments needed for children's spiritual nature to continue to thrive (see the figure "Phase 2: Spiritual Moments"). Together they create a system for spiritual development.

This system begins with five assumptions all supported by most participants in the study. The assumptions are

1. Spirituality is an inborn, human trait.

2. This innate trait must be nurtured to flourish. (Being in nature is one way to nurture spiritual development.)

3. Spiritual development is an important component of high-quality early childhood education.

4. More of the whole child is developed when spiritual development is supported in a young child's life.

5. Addressing spiritual development can lead to a better society.

Phase 1: Deep connections and dispositions. Phase 1 consists of three parts. The *first part,* deep connections, begins when children seek connections with others, with nature, and with big questions that are capable of taking children beyond oneself. The *second part* of phase 1 describes how basic dispositions are nurtured. Parents and educators first observe each child's disposition and then provide environments and moments capable of filling the child with wonder, awe, joy, and inner peace. These environments and moments will vary depending on the temperament, interests, and disposition of each child. The *third part* of phase 1 describes children's natural responses to everyday events after experiencing deep connections and having their basic dispositions nurtured. Participants described how children who frequently experience wonder, awe, joy, and inner peace are more likely to act with caring, kindness, empathy, and reverence. Participants also discussed how these acts or complex dispositions generate more and better relationships. The process is therefore self-renewing and viewed as a system.

Phase 1: Deep Connections and Dispositions

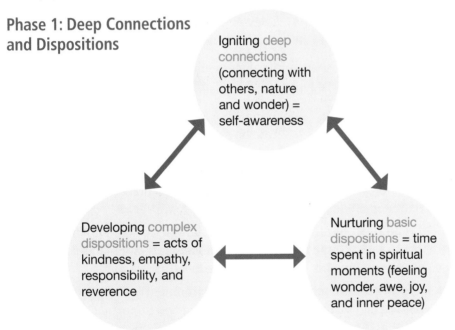

Phase 2: Spiritual moments. *Spiritual moments* (feeling wonder, awe, joy, and inner peace) is a concept that emerged from this study. It builds on the Reggio Emilia understanding of "the environment as a third teacher" (Edwards, Gandini, & Forman 2012, 149) and Schwab's concept of milieu. *Milieu* refers to the environment, situations, and surroundings as well the tonal qualities of a moment (Schwab 1969). Participants in the study described how children are capable of building deep connections if their learning environment supports spiritual moments in *time, space, nature, relationships,* and having big questions that are *beyond oneself.*

Phase 2: Spiritual Moments

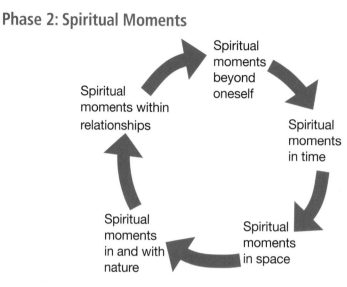

Participants described spiritual moments most frequently existing

* **In time**, meaning inclusive of routine, moments of quiet, and extended time to engage or focus in self-chosen activities

* **In space**, meaning that the space is beautiful, stimulating, organized, pleasing, and very important

* **In and with nature**, meaning that children are afforded much outdoor play and that natural objects and experiences are brought indoors for continued, in-depth exploration.

* **In relationships**, meaning that caring, kindness, and empathy (toward people and other living things, such as animals and plants) are part of the curriculum and are modeled by educators.

* **Beyond oneself,** meaning that the environment is designed so that children can begin to wonder and ask big and important questions that help them move beyond themselves

The idea of spiritual moments captures the environmental qualities that are necessary for nurturing children's spiritual development.

Spiritual Development and Nature Experiences

Unlike research on children's spiritual development, research on children and nature is abundant, although most studies focus on older children. Phenice and Griffore (2003) recorded the responses of children in a university-based laboratory preschool and a Head Start classroom. The children

One child's exploration with a flashlight led the whole school to start an investigation of light that lasted the school year. The project culminated with the creation of a chandelier made of prisms. The children are struck with wonder, awe, and joy of what light brings to the classroom. Their questions and appreciation of a world beyond themselves abound.

were asked a series of questions "about their perception of nature and their relationship to nature" (168). While most of the children readily identified trees and animals as part of nature, fewer identified plants and people as part of nature.

In my own study (Schein 2012) of spiritual development, adult participants spoke about spiritual moments in time. Young children require unhurried time to explore natural environments (Mustard 2006). They need to see what's in the environment, touch it, experiment with it, ask their own questions, and be given language to reinforce their experiences (Gardner 1999).

Five-year-olds Madeline and Jaden crawl among the plants in the garden of their early childhood program's outdoor classroom. "Look," Madeline says, "it's a ladybug. It's a crawling ladybug on a leaf." Jaden, an active, inquisitive child, reaches out to grab the insect. "Be careful," Madeline cautions softly. "Be very, very careful." In response to Madeline's urging, Jaden gently strokes the ladybug's back. "It's beautiful," he whispers (adapted from Rosenow 2011, 4)

As teachers record children's experiences and ideas about the outdoors, support and extend those ideas, and suggest ways for children to revisit their explorations, they help to build children's relationship with nature (Raikes & Edwards 2009; Rinaldi 2006).

Nature helps to calm and focus children, enabling them to form and strengthen those relationships with their world that are so important to their development. Sullivan, Kuo, and DePooter (2004) studied gardens and natural spaces near apartments and found that green spaces are capable

of bringing people together in relationships by providing outdoor areas for socializing. This study showed that nature plays an important role in creating neighborhoods. In Taylor and Kuo's (2008) study of children with attention-deficit/hyperactivity disorder (ADHD), the children were more focused and calmer after walking through a park. Kuo (2010), in a study on forests and recreation, found improved social, psychological, and physical well-being for those who spend time in nature.

Other studies show that a love of nature and a caring, ethical attitude toward the environment develop when children have regular time to play in and explore natural environments (Bailie 2010; Benson, Miller, & Leeper 2008; Davis 2009; Elliott 2006; Moore & Marcus 2008; Wilson 2012b). When environmental education includes experiences with nature (Moore and Marcus [2008] and Sobel [2004]), teachers can help children avoid developing a fear of the natural world and develop values that reflect a love for it.

Outdoor play is important because it offers children unstructured time to experience education as part of life rather than separate from it (Gardner 1991). Nature also offers varied opportunities for

The Great Outdoors

critical thinking and problem solving. Playgrounds should therefore stimulate children's natural curiosity, imagination, wonder, and desire to discover and learn; they should also nurture children's connections with nature (Moore & Marcus 2008).

Kellert (2005) contends that both physical and mental well-being depend on the quality and quantity of one's experience with the natural world. Kellert studied children's emotional, intellectual, and evaluative development—the latter referring to children's ability to form values, or attitudes, particularly in relation to the outdoor environment. Demonstrating a relationship between the natural world and emotional maturation, he used the five stages of emotional maturation outlined by Krathwohl, Bloom, and Masia (1964) to describe how children form values. Children move from *receiving* information and ideas about the environment to *responding* to the information and ideas, *valuing* them, *organizing* them, and, finally, to *developing their own philosophy* of life based on their emerging values and beliefs.

Kellert, along with Searles, Gardner, and Montessori, believes time in nature to be important to development. Spiritual development is intertwined with cognitive, social, emotional, and physical development as well as the development of values and an appreciation of the environment. It may even be the foundation for human development. Yet in his description of the status of nature education for young children in the United States in the twenty-first century, Kellert emphasizes that children lack opportunity to engage directly with nature.

Researchers using a variety of methodologies have linked high-quality early childhood education to nature education (Bailie 2010; Benson, Miller, & Leeper 2008; Davis 2009; Elliott 2006). Some specifically connect spiritual education to nature education (Kirmani & Kirmani 2009; Wilson 2012b). The participants in my study (Schein 2012) also referred to children's connectedness to nature as being profound and fundamental to their spiritual development, as indicated by this sampling of their observations:

> I think the environment plays a very important role in spiritual development. The environment can speak to a child about being valued, welcomed, and respected. It can tell a child that he or she is a competent, creative person. It can put a child in touch with beauty, a sense of the sacred, and connectedness with others.

> The environment [should have] . . . plants, and animals, and . . . lots of light. I think [we need] natural materials—wood, things that are not plastic, real things—that get us in touch with ourselves.

I feel strongly about [children] having close contact with nature. They need to be immersed in . . . pile(s) of leaves and the sand on the beach. Their involvement in nature should also include being active in the caring of these things and the caring of the natural world around them. This is one of the strongest ways to support spiritual development because there is that sense of beauty and mystery and that oneness in the natural world. By having children experience that in the natural world, it strengthens their spiritual development.

I spend a lot of time on the environment, and making sure that the environment is a place that is welcoming—really welcoming—a place that has beauty that relates to the child's way of understanding beauty and openness.

Because spiritual development is especially facilitated by nature, teachers have a responsibility to ensure that all children have daily, meaningful experiences with the natural world. As Rachel Carson (1965) counsels, for a child's sense of wonder to be kindled and kept alive, the child needs the "companionship of at least one adult who can share it, rediscovering with him the joy, excitement, and mystery of the world we live in" (45). Each of us can try to be that adult.

Interactions with other people and with our natural world give us a feeling of wholeness and a connection to what is beyond ourselves (Chawla 2012). This is what nature offers for humans of all ages.

The next chapter explores nature and outdoor play spaces for children in urban areas. Both the challenges and opportunities for connecting children with nature in urban environments, places where spiritual moments can continue to thrive, will be described.

Reflections

* How can I support children's spiritual development, which begins at birth and must be nurtured to foster the development of the whole child?

* How can I find new ways of viewing deep connections as defined in this chapter as connecting with others, nature, and wonder sources that nurture children's spiritual development?

* How can I help parents and early childhood educators become more aware of the importance of fostering children's spiritual moments in time, in space, with and in nature, in relationships, and through asking big questions that are capable of taking children beyond themselves?

* How can I help develop a shared language for discussing spiritual development? Deep connections and a sense of belonging, dispositions, and spiritual moments offer a beginning language for this important topic of development.

* How can I develop my own spirituality so I am a model for children?

What You Can Do

1. Nurture children's spiritual development by providing loving relationships and a loving environment.

   * Observe children closely to understand what interests them, then respect and encourage those interests. Record, review, and reflect on patterns that emerge. Use this to inform your understanding of each child's disposition. For example: "Leo always makes a beeline to the woods" . . . "Laura loves to play in sand."

   * Include families and other educators in a circle of positive relationships.

2. Create a learning environment with beautiful spaces made of natural materials. Select objects that reflect your observations of each child so the environment nurtures children's dispositions.

   * Bring a few of the children's outdoor discoveries indoors for in-depth exploration.

   * Keep your indoor environments simple, clean, beautiful, and well organized so children can make better choices as they look for materials.

* Fill beautiful baskets with natural materials such as acorns, pinecones, seashells, or seed pods. Place these baskets in front of windows, on top of colorful cloths, and on easy-to-access shelves for children to touch and explore.

* Replace plastic items with natural materials. For example, instead of using plastic bears for counting, provide acorns, pebbles, or seashells.

* Add flowers or plants such as a small spider plants.

* Consider including a pet, if permitted by your state regulations.

* Select each item with intentionality and purpose. Ask yourself, Which child will use this material?

3. Invite children to create artistic expressions of what they see in nature.

   * Let children draw what they see out in nature when they are outdoors and when they are indoors.

   * Provide clay and an array of art materials for children to explore the *hundred languages of children* by creating and reflecting upon their observations of nature and questions that arise from their observations. For example, if the children are observing and studying sunflowers, invite them to show their understanding of sunflowers by sketching or painting sunflowers or by creating with wire, collage, or clay.

4. Focus on deep connections. Help children explore aspects of the natural world in depth. Ponder with them. Extend their explorations. Encourage them to investigate to find answers to their questions. To know a few things deeply is often more satisfying than having a surface knowledge of many.

5. As children's questions about nature emerge, talk with and listen to what they have to say about their observations. Invite children to work together as they construct their knowledge about their discoveries.

Cities for Children

The word *city* may suggest images of concrete, traffic, and crowded streets, with little play space for children. Yet cities can have outdoor places that are nurturing and stimulating for children and also for adults. Do you have a favorite urban outdoor place?

A young teacher, Hayley, describes her favorite childhood urban space:

When I was very young, a place I loved was the tot-lot. I would play on the playground and walk around the huge open field where I always saw kids playing soccer as we drove by. I always wanted to be playing with them. Eventually, I became comfortable exploring different aspects of the tot-lot area and its surroundings. There was a thick wooded area behind it, and while I knew not to go in too far, I began to explore its opening.

The tot-lot was something different from my sheltered life. I realize it's a little strange that my memorable childhood experiences of expeditions were to a playground with woods that I probably went only three feet into. But something about that huge field, running around free, was amazing. Kicking the wood chips under my feet while I was swinging felt extraordinary. I loved it, and I continued to love it as I grew. If someone asked me to take them somewhere special, that's where I'd take them.

—Hayley Knudsen

Because more and more children live in urban areas, this chapter explores the challenges and opportunities of creating and keeping outdoor places for children. As Hayley's experience shows, children do not need wide open spaces to enjoy being outdoors.

The Context—Children and the Challenges Outdoors Today

Children thrive when they are in safe, stable places, so our challenge as individuals who care about children is to defend safe places, restore those that are neglected, and create new, hazard-free outdoor settings where children can play. Although it is surely true, as the Children's Defense Fund says, "The sea is so wide and my boat is so small."

Early childhood professionals are biased *toward* children. They find young children interesting, valuable, and worthy of time, money, attention, and care. But can the same be said of our nation's view toward children? Among the 40 richest, most developed nations of the world, the United States has nearly the highest percent of children who live below the poverty line (Stanford Center on Poverty and Inequality 2014). A 2012 study from the *Economist* Intelligence Unit (Watson 2012) showed that the United States ranks below the midpoint of 46 countries, both rich and poor, in providing a good start, affordable, high-quality preschools for young children. As we think about cities and how to make them better for children, it is important to recognize the condition of children's welfare in the United States. We have an uphill struggle, but working together we can achieve this goal.

Overall Context of Our Work With Children—Five Dimensions

Before describing examples of positive places and experiences for children in our cities and the people and organizations that are making them happen, we need to consider the larger context of our work with children. There are five main dimensions to keep in mind.

1. Land use is always contested, the more so when changes are proposed.

2. Our global population is steadily increasing, thus there are more children to take care of.

3. More and more people live in cities—globally, about 50 percent are urban dwellers and in the United States, about 80 percent (United Nations 2012).

4. In the United States, the income gap between the rich and the poor is increasing (Stone et al. 2013). Children are disproportionately among the poor (Stanford Center on Poverty and Inequality 2012).

5. Many economic policies and practices, in both rich and poor countries, hurt people and the environment (soil, air, water, plants, animals).

All of these factors affect the work of improving children's access to engaging, safe outdoor spaces.

1. Differing views over land use. Land is often viewed as a way to generate revenue—owners or developers make money from the development, sale, or leasing of land, and governments receive money from property taxes. Fortunately, zoning laws and environmental impact laws do offer some protections for citizens. Overall, though, families, teachers, and others may find it difficult to create and maintain safe spaces in which children can grow up. This chapter aims to strengthen your resolve to make a difference in the built environment—likely starting with your school or center and perhaps extending outward to the rest of the community.

One example of such involvement occurred a few years ago where I live in Bethesda, Maryland. A developer wanted to build a helipad on top of one of his new buildings. He also wanted an emergency landing pad on a piece of nearby "open space," which happened to be the elementary school playground. After parents and teachers objected to this use of the playground, the developer was forced instead to designate the flat roof of the neighborhood funeral home as the emergency landing spot. This was a relatively straightforward matter, but many land disputes are far more complicated and contentious. Although the process of contesting is complex and not necessarily enjoyable, we must make every effort to pursue matters that affect our children and our environment.

2. Increase in global population. The global population grew from 2 billion in 1950 to 7 billion in 2012 and is projected to reach 9.3 billion by 2050 (United Nations 2012). Water and food are already scarce in some areas. Will the world be able to provide for its inhabitants? Here in the United States, one in five children lives in poverty (United Nations 2012). Climate change, and the resulting record droughts and floods, is contributing to food shortages. Can our educational efforts and activism influence change?

3. More urban residents. According to the United Nations (2012), about 78 percent of the residents of developed countries, such as the United States, live in urban areas; in developing countries, the figure is 47 percent. By 2050, these numbers are projected to increase to 86 percent and 64 percent, respectively. Rural populations will likely decline. Large cities such as Los Angeles and New York with more than 10 million inhabitants will continue to grow, as will the number of urban dwellers who live in areas of fewer than 500,000 people (United Nations 2012). When so many people live in urban settings, the way cities function impacts education, health, and transportation.

As cities become more crowded, how do we preserve space for children? How do we make decision makers aware of children's space and safety needs? Schools and parks are often provided for children, but how about children's ability to move about, to be part of their community? In my town, which has changed from suburban to urban in the last 20 years, child care centers with small or no play yards have appeared. Open spaces that were once accessible to children have been built upon or otherwise developed with little attention given to children's needs.

4. Greater income gaps between rich and poor. The United States ranks third among all the advanced economies in the degree of income inequality (Organization for Economic Co-operation and Development 2013). The top one percent of Americans control nearly a quarter of the country's income, the highest share since 1928. Accompanying this has been a sorting of neighborhoods—people tend to live with others of similar income, which leaves the poorest people in the poorest neighborhoods where employment, schools, peers, and social networks are weakest (Weinberg 2011). In addition, low-income neighborhoods tend to have fewer trees, so they are warmer in the summer and have poorer air quality; they also generally offer fewer places for children to play safely outdoors (Zhu & Zhang 2008).

We must help rectify these situations. In *Blessed Unrest: How the Largest Social Movement in History Is Restoring Grace, Justice, and Beauty to the World* (2007), Paul Hawken describes many small-scale forces for good in the world

Stories From the Field:
Introducing Nature to Children in Urban Areas

One of the biggest challenges I've encountered is that children and adults have limited experience with nature. This can result in a fear of (or misinformation about) the natural world. Over the years I've introduced nature-based programs to many children in urban Head Start and child care centers. In most cases, the children, parents, and often the teachers had little experience being in natural spaces. Fear of the unknown or incorrect information (such as bears in the woods) was prevalent.

The best way to help urban children overcome their fears of the natural world and the animals who live in it is repeat visits to nature center habitats (at least once a month, if not more often), experience with animals in the wild, and, when possible, exploration of the outdoor spaces at their own school setting. Taking small steps, such as short hikes to familiar places, repeated visits with small animals (such as a turtle), and modeling appropriate behavior, is also important.

A good example of this approach was with a Head Start group in Cleveland, Ohio. We met twice a month, alternating between the nature center and the school. Every visit to the nature center included a chance to meet the resident box turtle. Initially the children were afraid of the turtle, but as they spent time with the turtle and learned that turtles have no teeth and eat many of the same foods that the children eat, things changed. When the children became familiar with the turtle, it gave them the confidence they needed to overcome their fears. When at the end of the year a new student was afraid of the turtle, the children encouraged her to not be afraid and shared with her what they knew about turtles. It was a remarkable experience and an amazing transformation of how the teacher and children viewed the natural world.

After the nine-month program was finished the teacher said, "I really like this nature stuff. How can I do what you do?" When we started the program, this teacher didn't like to go outside, but by the following year, she not only went outside, she knew how to dress for the cold winters. She also made sure that the children in her class were warm enough to go outside all year long.

—Patti Ensel Bailie, education director, The Biosophical Institute

and asserts that they are making a difference. Similarly, *Yes* magazine offers monthly encouragement with articles about individuals and small groups contributing to the larger good.

5. Damaging economic policies and practices. In the United States where there is a lot of land, and only 315 million of the world's 7 billion

people, the national economy has been based on extraction—taking things out of the ground like coal, oil, natural gas, copper, silver, gold, and other minerals, and leaving behind large toxic wastes, changed landscapes, and diminished habitats for the other creatures of the planet. In addition, in two or three generations in the United States, monocropping agribusinesses that rely heavily on chemical fertilizers and pesticides—which damage the soil, the water, and associated plants and wildlife—have replaced many self-balancing, sustainable operations farms. A pesticide seems to be implicated in the current die-off of bees that pollinate our crops (PANNA 2012). The Gulf of Mexico has a huge dead zone resulting from agricultural and urban runoff (National Oceanic and Atmospheric Administration [NOAA] 2009). What should we do and teach in these circumstances?

Early childhood education has a long history of local environmental activism: We encourage children and families to use water wisely, recycle trash, and turn off the lights. To truly effect change that will benefit children, however, we must expand our scope and consider what is going on around us and beyond us. We have some role models. As early as 1978, Lois Gibbs suspected that the reason why the children and adults in her community were sick was connected to the toxic wastes in the Love Canal in New York. Her activism to inform local, state, and national governments about the Love Canal ultimately resulted in the creation of the EPA's Superfund to clean up toxic waste sites in the United States. Erin Brockovich's certainty that something was wrong with the drinking water in Hinkley, California, impelled her to begin decades of activism. Ecologist Sandra Steingraber, alerted to environmental hazards at the age of 20 by her own pesticide-linked bladder cancer, has become fierce in noticing and navigating the environmental hazards her children now encounter. She writes at the end of *Raising Elijah: Protecting Our Children in an Age of Environmental Crisis* (2011) her account of making daily life accountable and sane:

> Ultimately the environmental crisis is a parenting crisis. It undermines my ability to carry out two fundamental duties: to protect my children from harm and to plan for their future. My responsibility as a mother thus extends beyond push mowers and clotheslines to the transformation of the nation's energy systems along renewable lines. Fine. With joy and resolve . . . I hereby devote myself to the task. When I watch my children breathing in their sleep, it doesn't feel like a choice. (281–82)

Early childhood educators have such responsibility as well.

The Promise—Child-Friendly Cities and Environments

UNESCO sponsored an international study of children growing up in cities in the 1990s, a reprise of a 1970s study. In the study, titled Growing up in Cities (GUIC) and headed by Louise Chawla (2002), teams of researchers interviewed and observed children in several cities as they worked and played. Cities from the United States, Australia, Argentina, India, South Africa, Poland, Norway, and Great Britain were included. Researchers worked in "old working class neighborhoods, peripheral suburbs, a self-built settlement, and a squatter camp" (Driskell 2002, 19). The overall findings of the multiyear, multisite study as summarized by Driskell (2002) showed that children valued

* Social integration

* A variety of interesting activity settings

* Safety and freedom of movement

* Peer meeting places

* Cohesive community identity

* Green areas

Around the world children want to feel that they are safe, are part of their neighborhoods and communities, and have the basics of clean water and sanitation. Older children want places to gather, and all want green spaces for play and gathering. Furthermore, children want to participate in decisions made about them. The United Nations Convention on the Rights of the Child (CRC) corroborates these findings.

Child-Friendly Cities

The GUIC study provides a framework for considering how to make cities places where children thrive. It has also contributed to the international movement to create "child-friendly cities," a movement that seeks to appropriately apply the CRC in cities and communities where children live.

> A child friendly city is the embodiment of the Convention on the Rights of the Child at the local level, which in practice means that children's rights are reflected in policies, laws, programmes and budgets. In a child friendly city, children are active agents; their voices and opinions are taken into consideration and influence decision-making processes. (UNICEF 2012)

UNICEF promotes a well-developed Child Friendly Cities Initiative (CFCI; see www.childfriendlycities.org/). The CFCI website describes positive, detailed Action Plans with Building Blocks, as well as research and case studies, to assist groups or individuals wishing to initiate action in their city or community.

The United States signed but has not ratified the CRC, nor does it have a specified child-friendly city. Nonetheless, the ideas contained in both resonate with much of early childhood theory and practice, as well as with contemporary thinking about children in general. The United States signed the CRC two decades ago, but Senate ratification is constitutionally necessary for it to become binding. There is an ongoing movement in the United States to have the Senate ratify the CRC; the website of the lead organization, Child Rights Campaign, is www.childrightscampaign.org/.

Children's Access to the Outdoors—Green Space Needed

Since the 1990s there has been a movement for "smart growth" to reduce suburban sprawl, encourage urban infill, and increase reliance on transit. Many of the results of this movement have been good for children, including a reduction in health-impairing pollution from vehicles. But when smart growth began two decades ago, the research showing how essential nature is to human health was scant. Now it is abundant and compelling (Kuo 2010). However, smart growth practices do not seem to have taken this new research into account; infilling, for example, has caused the loss of many potential play spaces. The biophilia principle—that people are an integral part of nature and cannot healthily be divorced from it—has yet to find a firm place in most city planning.

A DVD from the Environmental Protection Agency (EPA), "Wetlands and Wonder: Reconnecting Children With Nearby Nature" (2008), documents the loss due to infill of undeveloped neighborhood spaces where children used to play. (See http://water.epa.gov/type/wetlands/outreach/wetlands-video_index.cfm.) Ironically, some inner cities abandoned by industry and commerce offer potential play spaces in the form of vacant lots. Vacant lots that have been cleared of any hazards and retrieved by nature, and are located in safe areas, can be preserved as play spaces for children. Furthermore, these open spaces can be havens for beneficial wildlife as climate change affects animal habitats. More greenery improves the air quality and absorbs runoff. Daylighting, or redirecting creeks from underground culverts to more natural channels above ground, can also provide habitats for both children and wildlife. According to Chris Baines in *Urban Wildscapes* (2012):

> Urban wild space has a valuable role to play in tackling some of the great problems of today. Access to nature, environmental protection, healthy living, safer neighborhoods—they can all be achieved in part through a more positive approach to urban green space. (xv)

A study of sprawl's nega-
tive impact on biodiversity
in major metropolitan areas
of the United States under-
scores the point of protecting green spaces (Ewing &
Kostyack 2005). Children and
wildlife both need green infrastructure.

Play advocate Joan
Almon (pers. comm.) reminds
us of pieces of land that we
adults might have once loved
and emphasizes their value
for children, especially young
ones: "If we give children just
little bits, little remnants,
things that an adult would
cast away . . . to children
these are treasures that go
deep in their souls and last a
lifetime."

Repurposing green spaces. In some cities the demolition of abandoned homes has opened up wild green space. Among other cities, Detroit,
Michigan, has created gardens from large sections of open space. Often,
these new city gardens have open space for small children along the edges,
next to fences, and occasionally someone will plant a bean tepee for children. The venerable American Community Gardening Association has
extensive resources for supporting gardens, including modest grants for city
gardens (www.communitygarden.org).

Designing nature play spaces. There are many programs that seek
to identify, save, or build nature play spaces for young children in public
places. Nature play spaces generally include the native trees and shrubs of
a region—both as living specimens and as logs or loose parts—boulders
for climbing on, ponds and/or streams, and gardens of native flowers. The
Maryland Department of Natural Resources offers a pattern book of ideas
for natural play spaces, grouped by David Sobel's categories of outdoor
play (2008). It can be accessed at www.dnr.state.md.us/cin/nps. Columbus,
Ohio, provides a list of natural play spaces in its metro area parks
(www.metroparks.net/NaturalPlayAreas.aspx). Ken Finch (2009) takes a

realistic, practical approach to the process to establishing nature play spaces in nature centers or other public places and provides thoughtful guidelines for doing so (see www.greenheartsinc.org/uploads/Green_Hearts_Design_Principles_for_Nature_Play_Spaces.pdf).

The National Wildlife Federation (NWF) and the Natural Learning Initiative (NLI), along with several other partners, have collaborated to produce guidelines for designing natural play and learning areas that can be implemented in a variety of settings (scheduled for 2014). The guidelines are being piloting at several demonstration sites in cities around the country. See the Natural Learning website for the guidelines and updates: http://naturalearning.org/sites/default/files/Project_Registration_FINAL_0.pdf.

Should children "take only pictures, leave only footprints"? Teachers and naturalists often worry about children being careless or destructive to plants and small animals. Our efforts to encourage humane, compassionate behavior lead us to caution children against such actions. Finch, however, takes a practical view of minor damage to the environment that may occur as children play. (See sidebar "Don't Fear the Reaper.")

Sobel (2012), critiquing traditional environmental education, cites the immersive childhood play of noted naturalists John Muir, Aldo Leopold, and Edward O. Wilson and advises adults to let children follow their innate play instincts. "Nature programs should invite children to make mud pies, climb tree, catch frogs . . . get their hands dirty and their feet wet. They should be allowed to go off the trail and have fun" (67). Free play in nature during childhood often leads to caring and concern for nature in adulthood.

Pelo (2009) suggests a different approach. When the preschoolers she teaches encounter insects, she encourages imaginative storytelling about the insects. For instance, when she observes a child about to stomp on an ant with her foot, Pelo asks the child to imagine where that little ant is going. Is it going down under the sidewalk? Does it have a family down there? What are the family

Don't Fear the Reaper

Active, engaging nature play will cause damage or even death to some organisms. Plants will be uprooted, tree limbs will be broken off, butterflies will be caught and injured, ants will be fried with magnifiers, foxes will be scared away from potential den sites, etc. So what? These are not actions that will threaten the world's ecology. In fact, they will probably cause less cumulative ecological harm than did the creation of your building site, parking lot, entry road, and trails. They will *certainly* do less harm in a year than a bulldozer does in 10 minutes of groundwork for that new superstore down the road. Realize that these kinds of kid-caused damage to nature are an inherent part of nature play—and that nature play is a vital conservation strategy. Also realize that most such harm is not evil in intent, but rather is more akin to children performing simple, spontaneous science experiments. Kids need to learn how much impact they can have on other life forms, pro and con. [I] believe that this is a common part of the process of developing personal empathy for other life forms. Don't encourage it, but don't worry about it too much either.

Source: Reprinted by permission from K. Finch, "Design Principles for Nature Play Spaces in Nature Centers and Other Natural Areas," (Omaha, NE: Green Hearts Institute for Nature in Childhood, 2009), 3. www.greenheartsinc.org/uploads/Green_Hearts_Design_Principles_for_Nature_Play_Spaces.pdf.

members doing just now? The child absorbs the idea of the ant family and projects a happy life for the ants, for which she then wants to become the protector. Some teachers might prefer this model for interacting with children, even as they acknowledge the realism of Finch's view in "Don't Fear the Reaper" on page 82.

Revitalization of Parks as Green Space

The flourishing of suburban areas following World War II provided many families with their own green spaces—lawns—and reduced a natural constituency for public green space (Kelly Cook, pers. comm.) Many urban parks became untended and much city programming for children was abandoned (Kelly Cook, pers. comm.). Parkies, public employees who oversaw and facilitated children's play, were phased out. Even the condition of Central Park in New York City declined. Today there is only one park per 3,000 people (Trust for Public Land 2012). As urbanization increasingly overtakes open space, we must remedy this deficiency. Fortunately, many cities are focusing on parks again. This is good news for children, although we need to ensure that parks have natural spaces for children to explore. Both quality and quantity are at stake. The Trust for Public Land has a scoring system for parks, using the variables of access, funding (investment per resident, and number of playgrounds per 10,000 residents), and acreage (see ParkScore Index at www.parkscore.tpl.org/methodology.php).

Teardrop Park—a spectacular nature replication. A lovely park set on 1.8 acres between tall buildings in lower Manhattan, Teardrop Park is an artfully designed nature play space for children. Intended to portray all the topographies of New York State, it features stone cliffs, climbing boulders, brushy paths, waterfall and pond, and a sandy beach. Plants are all native species, and no pesticides or fertilizers are used. The award-winning playground is truly beautiful. (You can view photographs of it on the webpage of the architect, Michael Van Valkenburgh: www.mvvainc.com/project.php?id=2.)

Children's participation in park design. Teardrop Park was designed by experts, including Robin Moore, who advised the architect on child development principles and nature play. Reflecting his own belief in the CRC, however, Moore has also engaged children in creating their own park. The Kids Together Playground in Cary, North Carolina (kidstogethercary.org), represents a collaborative inclusive process for the city's children and is described by Moore & Cosco (2007b). Following the principles of universal design (Goltsman 2011), the playground encourages children of all abilities to play with one another while interacting with nature and playground equipment. The children chose the name Kids Together to reflect this. Ankenny, Iowa, offers another example in which the community was involved in planning parks and playgrounds. It is worth mentioning that more than good parks are achieved through this process— citizenship skills develop as well. Chawla (2002) observes, "Participation may serve extrinsic purposes in terms of concrete community improvements and more child-sensitive policies, but it also appears to foster an intrinsic sense of self-esteem and self-efficacy that is a basic preparation for citizenship" (234).

Early childhood professionals might wonder if young children can participate meaningfully in designing play spaces. Mindful that children are the "experts" in play, we can trust their instincts and encourage them to express their ideas. In *Creating Better Cities With Children and Youth: A Manual for Participation* (2002), Driskell notes that children can be surprisingly insightful. He advises:

> The most reliable way for ensuring that project objectives and activities are age-appropriate is to involve the children themselves in defining the project's objectives and determining its activities. The adult facilitator must ensure that objectives and activities can be achieved within the overall constraints of the project. (27)

Parks and playgrounds together. Research indicating that exercise space, green or not, will be used regularly if it is within a half mile of an adult has led at least two cities, St. Petersburg, Florida, and Tucson, Arizona, to aim at providing parks with playgrounds within a half mile of every resident. The idea is to offer opportunities for exercise for both children and adults (see www.stpete.org/outside/playgrounds.asp).

Jurisdictional boundaries often make play spaces inaccessible to children. Many schools, for example, lock their grounds after school and on weekends, preventing children from playing there during nonschool hours. To help remedy this problem, KaBOOM!, a nonprofit organization that helps communities of residents with low income build conventional playgrounds, has teamed with legal and policy experts to create *Playing Smart: Maximiz-*

ing the Potential of School and Community Property Through Joint Use Agreements. This detailed toolkit helps communities develop joint-use agreements for play spaces, such as schoolyards and parks, to maximize children's access to play facilities. The toolkit includes types of agreements in use around the country as well as a useful typology of funding sources (National Policy and Legal Analysis Network to Prevent Childhood Obesity, Public Health Law and Policy, & KaBOOM! 2012). In *Play Matters: A Study of Best Practices to Inform Local Policy and Process in Support of Children's Play* (2009), KaBOOM! honors cities that have joint-use agreements and other initiatives to extend and enhance children's access to play spaces.

Water's new prominence in parks. Perhaps the first nationally known park to feature water jets spurting up from the ground was in San Jose, California, in the mid-1990s. News stories noted that children were playing in the water. Such splash parks are now common. Los Angeles, for example, opened a new park in the civic center in 2012 with a huge "membrane pool" that is enjoyed by people of all ages.

Such pools are not the same as natural creeks and ponds, but water in any form is fun to play in.

Trails as green space for children. An encouraging development of the last decade has been increased attention to trails for walking and biking. Old railway beds in New York (The High Line), Philadelphia (The Reading Viaduct), Chicago (Bloomingdale Trail), Atlanta (Beltline Trail), Washington, DC (Capital Crescent Trail), and numerous other locations have been transformed from abandoned weed-filled spaces into linear urban parks. Unused railways have also become trails, such as the Great Allegheny Passage into Pittsburgh.

A program of the National Park Service—Rivers, Trails, and Conservation Assistance—helps communities establish nearby trails, because these trails are likely to be used and have an impact on community health and pleasure (National Park Service 2009). The program offers technical assistance in design, planning, and implementation (see www.nps.gov/rtca).

The United States is currently in the Decade of National Trails, which will culminate in the fiftieth anniversary of the National Trails System Act of 1968. The national trails system encompasses more than 60,000 miles of scenic, historic, and recreational trails (see www.Americantrails.org/resources).

A large regional cooperative project to build and connect trails was launched in 2007 in North and South Carolina. Named to invoke the history of the textile industry that once dominated the region's economy, the Carolina Thread Trail now links communities in both states with 135 miles of trails and more planned. The project aims at 100 miles in each county. "The Thread," as it is known, preserves historical and cultural sites, joins citizens in common effort, and provides exercise and education for nearly 2.3 million people. Private donations, public funds, and land donations support the project. See www.carolinathreadtrail.org.

Social integration. One of the findings of the Growing Up in Cities research mentioned previously in this chapter was that children want to feel part of the community in which they live, to feel welcome and valued. Children are sensitive to whether an environment welcomes them. A landmark study in England, which recorded the responses of children to photographs of various city places, showed that while children accepted streets in disarray they expressed sadness and anger that schoolyards—"their places"—were not better kept. Children felt disrespected (Titman 1994).

Some businesses find it profitable to be welcoming to children, as David Sucher points out in *City Comforts: How to Build an Urban Village* (2003). Children and parents alike appreciate appealing commercial establishments with child-friendly policies, shopping malls with play spaces, and public restrooms with diaper-changing facilities. Sucher suggests adding other child-friendly additions to public spaces, such as play graphics like hopscotch on pavement, pocket parks in shopping districts, and art that children can interact with. Sucher also advocates having many places to sit in public areas. They are good for tired little legs and good for adults, adding comfort along with a lively streetscape.

KaBOOM!, mentioned previously in this chapter, aims to create a playground within walking distance of every child in the United States. Following a tightly structured protocol, KaBOOM! and its corporate partners help residents of low-income neighborhoods organize themselves, including raising money, to build a conventional playground. In the design phase, children are invited to express their wants and suggestions for the playground. The planning results in a one-day event in which the playground is constructed. The community cooperation and the colorful structures that result indicate clearly to children that they are valued. In addition, the adults who work on the projects learn to work together and have something tangible to be proud of. Since 1995 KaBOOM! has built more than 2,200 playgrounds. Another Ka-BOOM! initiative is the searchable Map of Play, available both on the website (mapofplay.kaboom.org) and as an app to locate playgrounds in the United States and Canada. The app is also interactive; users can post photographs and comments. Furthermore, KaBOOM! helps communities develop Play Days and gain national recognition as Playful Cities USA for promoting play. More than 200 cities have been awarded the designation.

A new development in making children feel welcome is a movable play set that parks in a neighborhood for a day or so. Baltimore's Parks and People Foundation creates temporary play areas in outdoor spaces. Children use natural play loose parts, such as sticks, logs, straw, branches, and log slices, to play and create structures.

Imagination Playground in a Box has been part of some New York City parks since 2010. Portable carts deliver large, strong, blue foam pieces for children to play and build with. Additional materials can be added to the loose parts. The inventor of the materials, the Rockwell Group, is partnering with KaBOOM! to market them to playgrounds, children's museums, and elementary schools nationwide (Meade 2010). KaBOOM! offers competitive grants for the materials. See www.kaboom.org and www.imaginationplayground.com. It is heartening that new ideas for play are being implemented.

Children's Access to the Outdoors—Safety Needed

Our car-centric cities are being challenged by many factors, including the rising price of fuel, the realization that burning that fuel contributes to climate change, fatigue with long commutes and gridlocked traffic, the rising rate of obesity linked with lack of exercise, and a renewed popularity of bicycles as a preferred method of transportation. Thus early childhood educators wanting to make streets safer for children now have many allies. The following outlines a few effective traffic changes to make cities safer for children and for everyone.

Traffic calming. Traffic calming uses a variety of engineered solutions to make streets safer for residents, pedestrians, and cyclists. The practice is taking hold across the country and is something individuals in neighborhoods can help make happen. Several methods are used to slow vehicle traffic:

1. *Center islands of sufficient size for pedestrians and cyclists to be safe.* The photo shows how four car lanes were slimmed to two with a crossing island in the middle. Parents at a local school lobbied for 10 years to get these islands on this road to safeguard children's passage to the school on the other side.

2. *Speed bumps.* These humps in the road slow traffic on long, straight streets.

3. *Roundabouts.* These circular intersections have no traffic signals or stop signs, and traffic proceeds through the roundabout in a counter-clockwise direction. They are beneficial on straight streets where speed is an issue. They are less expensive than a stoplight and more responsive than a stoplight to variations in car volume, and reduce head-on vehicle accidents. Some designs are safer than others for pedestrians and cyclists, however.

4. *Corner bulbs.* These extensions of the sidewalk, also known as curb extensions, narrow the space for cars and extend the space for pedestrians. In some places they provide a bus stop. They make the crossing distance shorter for pedestrians and offer a better view of traffic.

Complete streets. "Complete streets" is a concept that holds that streets are "more than a way to move people in cars from point A to point B"; they provide for "safe access to destinations for everyone, regardless of age, ability, income, ethnicity, or mode of travel" (Smart Growth America & National Complete Streets Coalition 2012, 8). Thus a typical complete street would provide for use by pedestrians (e.g., a sidewalk), for bicyclists (e.g., designated lanes), the elderly (e.g., longer crossing times and islands in the middle of streets), children (e.g., bridges and tunnels for crossing busy thoroughfares), and persons with disabilities (e.g., crossings equipped with adaptive sounds and lights as well as sloped curbs). These examples are not exhaustive. Each community adapts the concept to its particular needs. As of the beginning of 2014, 610 jurisdictions in the United States had adopted policies for complete streets; jurisdictions including states, counties, cities, and communities (Smart Growth America and the National Complete Streets Coalition 2014).

The complete streets concept reduces the historical separation between vehicles and pedestrian/bicyclists. The concept facilitates communication and planning by recognizing that everyone needs to get around. An analysis and evaluation by Smart Growth America and the National Complete Streets Coalition (2014) can be read at www.smartgrowthamerica.org/documents/best-complete-streets-policies-of-2013.pdf. The report is a convenient resource to learn what is happening in your state or community.

A recent report on New York City's installation of complete streets has excellent photographs of what is in place there (see www.nyc.gov/html/dot/downloads/pdf/2012-10-measuring-the-street.pdf). This report also points out that when commercial streets are friendly to pedestrians and bikes, stores experience an increase in business because more people are moving more slowly.

The entire length of a street does not necessarily have to be complete. In cities such as San Francisco and Seattle, parts of numerous streets have been altered. Streets can be altered in a number of ways. One design that is used in urban areas changes four lanes of vehicle traffic into two lanes of traffic, a center turn lane, and a bicycle lane in each direction. This slows vehicle traffic down considerably, thus reducing accidents. Slower traffic is clearly good for children. Merchants prefer slower traffic as well, especially if the sidewalks are enhanced with parklets (parking spaces turned into parks) and outdoor tables and benches.

Residential and play streets. The residential street concept originated in northern Europe and has gained slow acceptance in the United States. Called a *woonerf* in the Netherlands, the residential street is shared by people and cars, with people setting the standard—cars cannot move faster than pedestrians. Cars are not allowed to use a disproportionate amount of space for parking. The street sign for a woonerf shows a pedestrian and a child playing. About two million people in the Netherlands live on such streets.

Play streets, more common in years past in the United States, are making a reappearance. In 2008, parents and activists in Jackson Park, part of the borough of Queens in New York City, gained permission to block off a street and extend a park on summer Sundays. The play street was so popular that in 2011 the supporters persuaded the city council to completely shut down the street during all of July and August. In 2012, the city agreed to develop the street into a plaza without traffic except for a pickup and drop-off area for the elementary school.

The process of citizen advocacy and action used to pursue the Queens play street is shown at www.streetfilms.org/a-car-free-street-grows-in-Queens. The video demonstrates the power of citizens to make changes for children. Persistence, courage, collaboration, and clear vision are critical elements. Another local citizen effort, in Menlo Park, California, is described in Mike Lanza's *Playborhood: Turn Your Neighborhood Into a Place for Play* (2012). Lanza, a parent of three young boys, was determined that his children would have fun outside the way he did as a child. So in a suburban neighborhood without large yards, he and his wife set up both their front and back yards to provide active play for children in the neighborhood. They enlisted their oldest child to look for playmates, lobbied their neighbors to join in, guided their oldest child to be independent on the quiet streets on his bike, held special activities, and generally transformed the neighborhood possibilities for play. Lanza is well aware of the importance of street safety and of having child-oriented neighbors—it does take a village. He is on a mission to bring play back to neighborhoods and his book offers many practical suggestions for doing so.

In late 2012 the Partnership for a Healthier America (PHA) and the BlueCross BlueShield Association joined in an initiative to create play streets across the United States. The plan is for ten cities to create at least four play streets each. The cities are Minneapolis, Minnesota; Savannah, Georgia; Durham, North Carolina; Buffalo, New York; New Orleans, Louisiana; York, Pennsylvania; San Francisco, California; Chicago, Illinois; Omaha, Nebraska; and Caguas, Puerto Rico. It is noteworthy that the main aim is reducing obesity in children, whereas the Queens project focuses on play and social interaction.

Safe Routes to School (SRTS) program. Founded in Denmark about 30 years ago, the Safe Routes to School program (Active and Safe Routes in Canada) has been operating in the United States since 2005 through federal legislation that gives block grants to the states. Most of the $1.1 billion from the federal government from 2005 to 2012 has gone to improve safety through infrastructure such as traffic calming, sidewalks, bike paths, crosswalks, and signage. Teaching children traffic safety skills, encouraging children to walk and bike to school, and directing drivers to drive safely around schools are also program elements. Funding was reduced in the 2012 legislation, although only 13,000 of the 99,000 public schools in the United States were participating (Safe Routes to School National Partnership 2012). Walking School Buses and Bike Trains are variant programs that have adult leadership, typically parents.

SRTS has attracted numerous partners because of its value. In addition to improved safety for children, the program is linked to

* Better air quality and improved health due to fewer emissions from cars and buses taking children to school

* Improved health from frequent exercise

* Reduced transportation costs for school districts

* Increased opportunities for socializing and community building

Parents and neighbors participate in conducting the program. Teachers can advocate for this program by contacting their representatives in Congress, their state and local departments of transportation, and their school principals and parent–teacher associations—each school makes the decision to participate. The SRTS program has an excellent website with detailed suggestions on advocating for and achieving safe routes to school. See http://guide.saferoutesinfo.org/introduction/index.cfm.

Encouraging biking to school through technology. Seeing that his children did not want to bike to school, in 2008 a tech-savvy father in Boulder, Colorado, devised the Freikur (for "frequent biker") program, which encouraged children to bike every day. Now called Boltage (www.boltage. org), the program features a solar-powered tracking device near the school that reads identifying chips on children's backpacks to keep track of trips made and miles accomplished. Reports are produced for each child as well as for the school and can be posted for school initiatives. The data-driven program is used in several cities. SRTS funds can be used for the equipment and incentives.

Getting About—Connected Communities

Children need access to more in their neighborhoods and communities than just their homes and schools. As children get older, they want to go places in their neighborhoods. Primary-age children learn to navigate their neighborhoods, often by accompanying older children. The skill of "wayfinding" is an evolutionary skill, linked with hunting and gathering, and learned from doing (Heerwagen & Orians 2002). Finding one's way around home and school by biking, walking, and exploring builds independence and mental mapping.

Walkable communities. Light rail transit (LRT), along with vehicle rapid transit (VRT), are increasingly seen as ways to manage urbanization. Because access to mass transit makes it possible to get around without driving everywhere, LRT, VRT, and other mass transit systems are at the core of the national movement to create walkable communities, ones in which most of life's daily necessities are within a short walk or short ride on mass transit. In the Washington, DC, area there are more than 34 such areas, most of which have grown up around subway stations. To learn how accessible an area is, you can locate a "walkscore" for any address at www.walkscore.com. More helpful is the Walkability Checklist, which is easily completed by taking a walk around your neighborhood and school (see http://katana.hsrc.unc.edu/cms/downloads/walkability_checklist.pdf). After completing this

basic research, use "A Residents' Guide to Creating Safe and Walkable Communities" for specific advice on identifying problems, seeking allies, locating professional agencies, understanding the processes for change, and identifying resources. See http://safety.fhwa.dot.gov/PED_BIKE/ped_cmnity/ped_walkguide/residentsguide.pdf.

I live in what is now currently termed

a "walkable community." A few examples show that planners have had children in mind. A plaza with apartments, small stores, and an attractive water feature that allows children to wade and climb on rocks is connected with a footbridge to the other side of the highway where there is a lawn, more apartments, and a child care center. This area in turn connects via another footbridge to a second plaza with a hotel and entrance to the subway below.

Another highway through the town has an elementary school, sports field, public library, park, and big grocery store all on the same side so that children have only less-busy streets to navigate. This town also has an abandoned railway trail that goes under two state highways, providing safe passage to shopping districts, six schools, and two child care centers with small play yards that are supplemented by the nature trail. A million walkers and bikers use this trail each year.

Complete communities. Children are not a specific focus in the development of walkable communities, but many urban planning groups are proposing a vision of transit-oriented neighborhoods and regions called complete communities, and this vision does consider children. The idea is to remedy the post-WW II zoning model that separates work and living, which has resulted in tremendous suburban sprawl and hollowed-out inner cities. Complete communities propose revitalizing urban and close-in suburban neighborhoods served by transit—for example, subways and light rail—to create highly walkable communities. Schools, parks, health facilities, apartments, houses, libraries, office buildings, retail, entertainment, and services of all kinds would compose the complete community. An important part of this concept is that residents already living in these neighborhoods are not pushed out by redevelopment; gentrification is prevented through strong zoning and provision for affordable housing (Sutton & Kemp 2011). It is important for children to have neighborhoods where adults are working and where amenities and services are offered. Complete communities are a well-developed and democratic form of walkable communities.

While transit is key to complete communities, building it is very expensive and complex. Typically several layers of government are involved in the planning, design, and building of transit projects. The US Department of Transportation dedicates funds to transit projects, but they are cost-sharing funds that keep the local and state governments in the picture. To help citizens participate in the process, Transportation for America has developed a toolkit, *Thinking Outside the Farebox: Creative Approaches to Financing Transit Projects* (http://t4america.org/wp-content/uploads/2012/08/T4-Financing-Transit-Guidebook.pdf).

Biophilic cities. Complete communities include access to nature in parks, but a biophilic city puts nature at the forefront. Beatley defines it as a city that "puts nature first in its design, planning and management; it recognizes the essential need for daily human contact with nature as well as the many environmental and economic values provided by nature and natural systems" (2011, 45). Preserving and restoring desirable natural features, such as views, creeks, and forests; using natural processes for heating, cooling, and waste management; reducing reliance on cars; linking green areas; and other locally appropriate methods are characteristics of biophilic cities.

How does such a city specifically enhance children's outdoor play? A study of biophilic Boulder, Colorado (Derr & Lance 2012), identifies how some natural elements are particularly useful to children, who can make a world in a small space. Open, flowing creeks with low banks, along with sticks and stones, are highly prized play spaces. A small pond at the library elicits water play and observation. Tall, dry grasses at the edge of a playing field become hiding places. A small tree inside the children's reading room at the library, intended for dappling light and dropping leaves, also invites climbing. Boulders placed in a street mall offer climbing and clambering experiences. Children everywhere invariably seek play spaces, and in the abundant natural features of Boulder, they find many. Can we make more cities biophilic?

Health Impact Assessment

Health Impact Assessments (HIAs), which are now used across the country, are an important advocacy tool that can be used to make cities more healthy. They are a relatively new variant on the environmental impact assessment required since the 1970s for land development projects. An HIA engages multiple stakeholders in a process to determine the impact of a proposed project on them. In the case of the trail near my home that I care about so much, the transportation department's views would be complemented by those of bicyclist groups, the county health department, pediatricians who prescribe outdoor exercise for children, citizens who live along the trail and are concerned about noise, the Safe Routes to School group, and perhaps others. In Northern European countries and in New Zealand, which have ratified the UN CRC, there is a Children's Impact Assessment (CIA) or a Child's Rights in Impact Assessment (CRIA) process. These child-focused assessments are used when the project being discussed is not specifically for children yet would impact them. The Robert Wood Johnson Foundation and the Pew Charitable Trusts fund some HIAs to increase their use (www.healthimpactproject.com), and the Centers for Disease Control and Prevention (CDC) recommends their use to communities (www.cdc.gov/healthyplaces/hia.htm). The HIA/CIA can be useful tools to focus on children's welfare.

This chapter offers suggestions for individual or group action focused on improving cities in the near term. For a longer view of increasing the positive aspects of urbanization, we can turn for inspiration to the article "Our Children's Cities: The Logic and Beauty of a Child-Centered Civilization," written in 2011 by Jason McLennan, a visionary architect.

Setting Priorities

McLennan asserts that if we make our cities good for children, cities will be good for all of us (2011). Cities are changing, for better or ill, so we should guide the change to meet children's needs, because children are our most vulnerable citizens as well as the inhabitants of the future. Noting that North American cities have been built around

cars, McLennan calls instead for building them around all people, including children. This vision includes low buildings and walkable communities. He believes that small cities can serve children well.

McLennan envisions what a child-centered city would include. Like the complete communities discussed in this chapter on page 93, a child-centered city would have a mix of families and incomes, with enough space for play and quiet, and a healthy mix of services and basic amenities. Like biophilic cities, it would also have "an abundance of nature—features that can offer both practical and environmental advantages while giving children easy access to clean water, climbable trees, and fresh air. . . . The idea here is to call upon nature to do double duty, providing amenities that also support urban infrastructure" (McLennan 2011, 33). Finally, the city would offer an abundance of recognized teaching opportunities in both the natural and built environment: "Teachers and children need only to step outside their classrooms and pay close attention to . . . the science, art, math, and music that surrounds them" (33). Other adults would help teach by making their occupations visible to the children, leading to a bond and trust between generations.

McLennan's vision is both appealing and practical. It does require that we stop regarding land solely as a commodity to be bought and sold and consider it instead as *our* place, *our* habitat, where we and our children and our broadly conceived, democratic communities live and thrive.

Reflections

* Does this chapter make you feel hopeful? What are some of the encouraging signs that you see in your community?

* Does this chapter make you feel overwhelmed? I sometimes feel that way. The good thing is that lots of people are trying to improve cities.

* Which aspect of urban living interests or concerns you? What do you plan to do about it?

What You Can Do

1. To make cities better for children, plant trees or create gardens in play yards or participate in community gardens.

2. To make cities better for everyone, support taxes to rebuild cities.

3. Become interested in plans for your immediate neighborhood. Do what you can to make them better for children.

4. Be alert to proposed changes in parkland, trails, and wetlands. Sometimes this land, which is valuable for children and as part of our ecosystems, becomes available for development, resulting in the disappearance of places where children can explore and play.

5. To make it possible for children to walk to school, contact your local school district to ask about the Safe Routes to School (SRTS) program. The SRTS website has a detailed and helpful guide about implementing the program (http://guide.saferoutesinfo.org). Help start a program, if there is not one already in place. Because grants for this program are awarded by the federal government to individual states, the place to contact is your state transportation department. In addition, consider getting in touch with your US Congress representative or senator to ask for increased federal funding for the SRTS program.

6. Take an interest in transportation projects, especially ones that help cars go faster, because slower cars are safer for everyone.

7. Advocate for complete streets in your community. Consult "A Resident's Guide to Creating Safe and Walkable Communities" available at http://safety.fhwa.dot.gov/PED_BIKE/ped_cmnity/ped_walkguide/index.cfm for resources and specific advice about identifying problems, seeking allies, locating professional agencies, and understanding the processes for change.

8. Stay on top of major transportation projects in your area. Look at Transportation for American's toolkit, *Thinking Outside the Farebox: Creative Approaches to Financing Transit Systems* at http://t4america.org/wp-content/uploads/2012/08/T4-Financing-Transit-Guidebook.pdf. Major transit projects require years of planning and negotiating, which means that there are many opportunities to voice your concerns.

Appendix

Background to the Problem of Pesticides and Other Toxins

As an environmentally minded teacher and parent, over the years I increasingly wondered why, when we *knew* that pesticides were poison, labeled with a skull and crossbones and a "Keep out of reach of children" warning, did we keep using them in homes and schools and parks? Why did we keep on allowing this, especially as research on pesticides reported in the popular press grew more alarming? I finally focused on this question during a sabbatical in 2010, attending Congressional hearings, writing comments for Environmental Protection Agency (EPA) regulatory hearings, and studying the history of federal regulations. This appendix outlines my understanding of the US government's role in the regulation of pesticides and other toxicants. I hope it is useful.

At present, there are more than 80,000 human-created chemicals in our air, water, and soil (Schafer 2012). The effects of most of them, alone and especially in combination with others, are not well understood or documented. Hundreds of studies here and abroad have shown that these chemicals have many negative effects including cancer, neurological and immune disorders, asthma, and obesity (Hotchkiss et al. 2008; Vandenberg et al. 2012). Similarly, their effect on developing organisms—fetuses, infants, and children—is not well known. A miniscule bit of exposure for an infant to a pesticide or other toxin may have effects that manifest much later in development, even to old age. In regard to pesticides, even common sense tells us that poison for animals is also poison for children. "Cide," after all, means "kill." Yet regulatory reform is very hard come by. The politics and complexities of toxicant research and regulation are beyond the scope of this book but are easy enough to research. Resources that have helped me understand the ongoing and severe problems are listed in the bibliography (Carson 1962; Cone 2005; Davis 2002; Ross & Amter 2010; Shabecoff & Shabecoff 2008; Steingraber 2010).

Many ordinary citizens know or sense at least that some substances are harmful. However, even after lead was identified as toxic, it still made car engines run more smoothly and improved paint, so it was accepted. DDT protected World War II soldiers from mosquitoes, and then it was applied widely to kill all manner of insects after that war. Again most people accepted this, if warily. But after the publication of Rachel Carson's *Silent Spring* (1962) that documented what widespread use of DDT did to all life, and after the Cuyahoga River in Cleveland caught fire in 1969, enough people in the United States focused on the real dangers of toxicants. Thus, with widespread bipartisan support, Congress in 1970 established the US Environmental Protection Agency (EPA), and passed the Clean Air and Clean Water laws, as well as regulations protecting health and the environment regarding insecticides, fungicides, rodenticides, and other toxins (Federal Insecticides, Fungicides, and Rodenticides Act, FIFRA, originally 1947 but rewritten in 1972), and other toxics (Toxic Substances Control Act, TSCA, 1976.)

The EPA's main method of determining whether a chemical is harmful to the environment or humans has been to intentionally administer it to experimental animals. This "risk assessment" practice has proved increasingly unsatisfactory in that 1) it takes a long time and is expensive, 2) it does not account for interactions of the increasing number of chemicals already in the organism, and 3) *it does not take account of the developmental or long-term effects of the chemical*. A miniscule bit, perhaps just a molecule, of a substance encountered by a fetus, can affect development far in the future, perhaps at puberty or in child-bearing years (Grandjean & Landrigan 2014).

Furthermore, young children are especially vulnerable to chemicals in that they are closer to the ground where chemicals end up, they put objects in their mouths as a way of learning about their environment, they breathe more air and eat more food for their size than adults do, and they are growing up—their nervous systems, their immune systems, their bodies, and their cognitive capacities are all developing.

Acknowledging children's extra vulnerabilities, an important National Research Council report "Pesticides in the Diet of Infants and Children" (1993), spurred additional federal legislation requiring that children be considered with much broader margins for safety (Food Quality Protection Act, FQPA, 1996). Children are not exposed to all chemicals, but all children consume food, so the pesticide residues on food are a significant concern. Children (and workers) who live where pesticides are being applied to food crops are at extra risk.

To improve the old, flawed risk-assessment model, the EPA in 2007 began to adopt a more sophisticated system, "The US Environmental Protection Agency's Strategic Plan for Evaluating the Toxicity of Chemicals," to identify and study "toxicity pathways," to see how cells respond to chemical "perturbation" (EPA 2011). The EPA states:

> The new paradigm should facilitate evaluating the susceptibility of different life-stages and genetic variations in the population, understanding the mechanisms by which toxicity occurs, and considering the risks of concurrent, cumulative exposure to multiple and divers chemicals, while at the same time significantly reducing reliance on animal testing for assessing human risk. (EPA 2011)

This strategic plan is promising although the implementation is challenging.

In addition, since 2010 Congress has been locked in a largely partisan struggle to rewrite the outdated Toxic Substances Control Act (1976), an important provision of which would require manufacturers to take the responsibility to prove their products are safe. It is a cause worth our close notice. A 2013 film, "The Human Experiment," documents aspects of the struggle (see www.thehumanexperimentmovie.com).

References

American Academy of Pediatrics (AAP). 2012a. "Fighting Vitamin D Deficiency." www.aap. org/en-us/about-the-aap/aap-press-room/aap-press-room-media-center/Pages/Fighting-Vitamin-D-Deficiency.aspx.

American Academy of Pediatrics (AAP). 2012b. "A Parent's Guide to Insect Repellents." http://patiented.aap.org/content2.aspx?aid=5556&refURL=.

American Academy of Pediatrics (AAP). 2012c. "Sun and Water Safety Tips." www.aap. org/en-us/about-the-aap/aap-press-room/news-features-and-safety-tips/Pages/Sun-and-Water-Safety-Tips.aspx.

American Academy of Pediatrics (AAP). 2013a. "The Crucial Role of Recess in School." Policy statement. *Pediatrics* 131 (1): 183–88. http://pediatrics.aappublications.org/content/131/1/183.full.

American Academy of Pediatrics (AAP). 2013b. "Safety in the Sandbox." www.healthychildren.org/English/safety-prevention/at-play/pages/Safety-in-the-Sandbox.aspx.

American Academy of Pediatrics, American Public Health Association, & National Resource Center for Health and Safety in Child Care and Early Education. 2011. *Caring for Our Children: National Health and Safety Performance Standards; Guidelines for Early Care and Education Programs. 3rd ed.* Elk Grove Village, IL: American Academy of Pediatrics; Washington, DC: American Public Health Association. http://cfoc.nrckids.org/WebFiles/CFOC3-color-small.pdf.

American Public Health Association (APHA). 2013. "Improving Health and Wellness Through Access to Nature." Policy statement. www.apha.org/advocacy/policy/policy-search/default.htm?id=1453.

Anggard, E. 2010. "Making Use of 'Nature' in an Outdoor Preschool: Classroom, Home and Fairyland." *Children, Youth and Environments* 20 (1): 4–25.

Armitage, K.C. 2009. *The Nature Study Movement: The Forgotten Populizer of America's Conservation Ethic.* Lawrence, KS: University Press of Kansas.

Australian Institute of Health and Welfare & Australasian Association of Cancer Registries. 2012. "Cancer in Australia: An Overview, 2012." Canberra: Australian Institute of Health and Welfare. www.aihw.gov.au/WorkArea/DownloadAsset.aspx?id=60129542353.

Bailie, P.E. 2010. "From the One-Hour Field Trip to a Nature Preschool Partnering With Environmental Organizations." *Young Children* 65 (4): 76–82.

Bailie, P.E. 2012. "Connecting Children to Nature: A Multiple Case Study of Nature Center Preschools." PhD diss., University of Nebraska–Lincoln.

Bailie, P.E., & K. Finch. Forthcoming. "Nature Preschools: Putting Nature at the Heart of Early Childhood Education." In *Developing Environmental Awareness in Children: A Nature Studies Guide for Parents and Educators,* eds. M.L. Bentley & M.P. Mueller. New York: Peter Lang.

Baines, C. 2012. "Foreword: The Wild Side of Town." *Urban Wildscapes.* New York: Routledge.

Balk, S.J. 2011. "Ultraviolet Radiation: A Hazard to Children and Adolescents." Technical report. *Pediatrics* 127 (3): 791–817. pediatrics.aappublications.org/content/127/3/e791.full.

Banning, W., & G. Sullivan. 2011. *Lens on Outdoor Learning.* St. Paul, MN: Redleaf Press.

Baumgartner, J.J., & T. Buchanan. 2010. "Supporting Each Child's Spirit." *Young Children* 65 (2): 90–95.

Beatley, T. 2011. *Biophilic Cities: Integrating Nature Into Urban Design and Planning.* Washington, DC: Island Press.

Benson, J., J.L. Miller, & J. Leeper. 2008. "Experiences in Nature: A Pathway to Standards." *Young Children* 63 (6): 22–28.

Berry, T. 1999. *The Great Work: Our Way Into the Future.* New York: Bell Tower.

Beyond Pesticides. 2012. "How to Repel Mosquitoes Safely." Accessed October 12. www.beyondpesticides.org/mosquito/documents/LesstoxRepellents.pdf.

Blain, M., & S. Eady. 2002. "The WOW Factor: Spiritual Development Through Science." *Westminster Studies in Education* 25 (2): 124–35.

Bleeker, M., S. James-Burdumy, N. Beyler, A.H. Dodd, R. London, L. Westrich, K. Stokes-Guinan, & S. Castrechini. 2012. "Findings From a Randomized Experiment of Playworks: Selected Results From Cohort 1." Report prepared for the Robert Wood Johnson Foundation by Mathematica Policy Research and Stanford University's John W. Gardner Center for Youth and Their Communities. www.mathematica-mpr.com/publications/pdfs/education/playworks_brief1.pdf.

Bogden, J.F., M. Brizius, & E.M. Walker. 2012. "Policies to Promote Physical Activity and Physical Education." Chap. D in *Fit, Healthy, and Ready to Learn: A School Health Policy Guide.* 2nd ed. Arlington, VA: National Association of State Boards of Education (NASBE). www.nasbe.org/wp-content/uploads/FHRTL_Physical-Activity-NASBE-Nov20121.pdf.

Buber, M. 1923 [1996]. *I and Thou* (W. Kaufmann, trans.). New York: Touchstone.

Bucklin-Sporer, A., & R.K. Pringle. 2010. *How to Grow a School Garden.* Portland, OR: Timber Press.

Bullard, R.D., P. Mohai, R. Saha, & B. Wright. 2007. *Toxic Wastes and Race at Twenty, 1987–2007: A Report Prepared for the United Church of Christ, Justice and Witness Ministries.* www.ucc.org/assets/pdfs/toxic20.pdf.

Carlson, F.M. 2006. *Essential Touch: Meeting the Needs of Young Children.* Washington, DC: NAEYC.

Carson, R.L. 1962. *Silent Spring.* Boston, MA: Houghton Mifflin.

Carson, R.L. 1965. *The Sense of Wonder.* New York: Harper & Row.

Centers for Disease Control and Prevention (CDC). 2002. *Shade Planning for America's Schools.* Atlanta, GA: CDC. www.cdc.gov/cancer/skin/pdf/shade_planning.pdf.

Centers for Disease Control and Prevention (CDC). 2010. *State Indicator Report on Physical Activity, 2010.* Atlanta, GA: US Department of Health and Human Services. www.cdc.gov/physicalactivity/downloads/PA_State_Indicator_Report_2010.pdf.

Centers for Disease Control and Prevention (CDC). 2012a. "CDC Response to Advisory Committee on Childhood Lead Poisoning Prevention Recommendations in 'Low Level Lead Exposure Harms Children: A Renewed Call of Primary Prevention.'" www.cdc.gov/nceh/lead/ACCLPP/CDC_Response_Lead_Exposure_Recs.pdf.

Centers for Disease Control and Prevention (CDC). 2012b. "Low Level Lead Exposure Harms Children: A Renewed Call for Primary Prevention." Report of the Advisory Committee on Childhood Lead Poisoning and Prevention of the CDC. www.cdc.gov/nceh/lead/ACCLPP/Final_Document_030712.pdf.

Centers for Disease Control and Prevention (CDC). 2012c. "Sunburn and Sun Protective Behaviors Among Adults Aged 18–29 years—United States, 2000–2010." *Morbidity and Mortality Weekly Report* 61(18): 317–22. www.cdc.gov/mmwr/preview/mmwrhtml/mm6118a1.htm.

Centers for Disease Control and Prevention (CDC). 2013. *Fourth National Report on Human Exposure to Environmental Chemicals. Updated Tables, September 2013.* Atlanta, GA: CDC. www.cdc.gov/exposurereport/pdf/FourthReport_UpdatedTables_Sep2013.pdf.

Chawla, L., ed. 2002. *Growing Up in an Urbanising World.* London: UNESCO & Earthscan.

Chawla, L. 2006. "Learning to Love the Natural World Enough to Protect It." *Barn* 2: 57–78.

Chawla, L. 2012. "The Importance of Access to Nature for Young Children." *Early Childhood Matters* 118: 48–51. vps.earlychildhoodmagazine.org/wp-content/uploads/2012/07/ECM118_11_The-importance-of-access-to-nature_Louise-Chawla.pdf.

Chawla, L., & V. Derr. 2012. "The Development of Conservation Behaviors in Childhood and Youth." In *The Oxford Handbook of Environmental and Conservation Psychology,* ed. S.D. Clayton, 527–55. New York: Oxford University Press.

Children and Nature Network & IUCN Commission on Education and Communication. 2012. *Children and Nature Worldwide: An Exploration of Children's Experiences of the Outdoors and Nature With Associated Risks and Benefits.* Minneapolis, MN: Children and Nature Network. www.childrenandnature.org/downloads/CECCNNWorldwideResearch.pdf.

Clements, R. 2004. "An Investigation of the State of Outdoor Play." *Contemporary Issues in Early Childhood* 5 (1): 68–80.

Coley, R.L., T. Leventhal, A.D. Lynch, & M. Kull. 2013. "Relations Between Housing Characteristics and the Well-Being of Low-Income Children and Adolescents." *Developmental Psychology* 49 (9): 1775–89.

Cone, M. 2005. *Silent Snow: The Slow Poisoning of the Arctic.* New York: Grove Press.

Copple, C., & S. Bredekamp, eds. 2009. *Developmentally Appropriate Practice in Early Childhood Programs Serving Children From Birth Through Age 8.* 3rd ed. Washington, DC: NAEYC.

Cowell, R. 2012. "In Their Backyard: Robert D. Bullard on the Politics of Where We Put Our Trash." *The Sun,* 437, May, 4S–10.

Danks, S.G. 2010. *Asphalt to Ecosystems: Design Ideas for Schoolyard Transformation.* Oakland, CA: New Village Press.

Dargan, A., & S. Zeitlin. 1990. *City Play.* New Brunswick, NJ: Rutgers University Press.

Davis, D. 2002. *When Smoke Ran Like Water: Tales of Environmental Deception and the Battle Against Pollution.* New York: Basic Books.

Davis, J. 2009. "Revealing the Research 'Hole' of Early Childhood Education for Sustainability: A Preliminary Survey of the Literature." *Environmental Education Research* 15 (2): 227–41.

Derr, V., & K. Lance. 2012. "Biophilic Boulder: Children's Environments That Foster Connections to Nature." *Children, Youth and Environments* 22 (2): 112–43. www.colorado.edu/journals/cye/22_2/22_2_06_Biophilic_Boulder.pdf.

Dewey, J. 1900/1902 [1990]. *The School and Society and The Child in the Curriculum.* Chicago, IL: University of Chicago Press.

Diaz, A., R.E. Neale, M.G. Kimlin, L. Jones, & M. Janda. 2012. "The Children and Sunscreen Study: A Crossover Trail Investigating Children's Sunscreen Application Thickness and the Influence of Age and Dispenser Type." *Archives of Dermatology* 148 (5): 606–12.

Driskell, D. 2002. *Creating Better Cities With Children and Youth: A Manual for Participation.* London: UNESCO & Earthscan.

Edwards, C., L. Gandini, & G. Forman, eds. 2012. *The Hundred Languages of Children: The Reggio Emilia Experience in Transformation.* 3rd ed. Santa Barbara, CA: Praeger.

Elliott, S. 2006. "Beyond Patches of Green: A Turning Point in Early Childhood Environmental Education." Paper presented at the Biennial Conference of the New Zealand Association of Environmental Education, Auckland, New Zealand.

Environmental Working Group. 2009. "Pollution in Minority Newborns: BPA and Other Cord Blood Pollutants." www.ewg.org/research/minority-cord-blood-report/bpa-and-other-cord-blood-pollutants.

Etzioni, A. 2001. *Next: The Road to the Good Society.* New York: Basic Books.

Ewing, R, & J. Kostyack, With D. Chen, B. Stein, & M. Ernst. 2005. *Endangered by Sprawl: How Runaway Development Threatens America's Wildlife.* Washington, DC: National Wildlife Federation, Smart Growth America, and NatureServe. www.nwf.org/pdf/Wildlife/EndangeredbySprawl.pdf.

Fenner, P.J., & K.L. Rivers, eds. 1992. *Waldorf Education: A Family Guide.* Amesbury, MA: Michaelmas Press.

Finch, K. 2009. *Design Principles for Nature Play Spaces in Nature Centers and Other Natural Areas.* Omaha, NE: Green Hearts Institute for Nature in Childhood. www.greenheartsinc.org/uploads/Green_Hearts_Design_Principles_for_Nature_Play_Spaces.pdf.

Fowler, J.W. 1995. *Stages of Faith: The Psychology of Human Development and the Quest for Meaning.* New York: HarperCollins.

Gammon, C. 2012. "Asthma and the Inner City: East St. Louis Children Struggle With Life-Threatening Disease." Part 8, Pollution, Poverty, and People of Color series. *Environmental Health News* (June 19). www.environmentalhealthnews.org/ehs/news/2012/pollution-poverty-people-of-color-asthma-and-the-inner-city.

Gandini, L., L. Hill, L. Cadwell, & C. Schwall. 2005. *In the Spirit of the Studio: Learning From the Atelier of Reggio Emilia.* New York: Teachers College Press.

Gardner, H. 1991. "The Tensions Between Education and Development." *Journal of Moral Education* 20 (2): 113–25.

Gardner, H. 1993. *Frames of Mind: The Theory of Multiple Intelligences.* New York: Basic Books.

Gardner, H. 1999. *Intelligence Reframed: Multiple Intelligences for the 21st Century.* New York: Basic Books.

Gardner, H., M. Csikszentmihalyi, & W. Damon. 2001. *Good Work: When Excellence and Ethics Meet.* New York: Basic Books.

Gerdes, J., & J.L. Miller. 2011. "Experiences in Nature: A Pathway to Standards." In *Spotlight on Young Children and Nature*, ed. A. Shillady, 24–30. Washington, DC: NAEYC.

Giesenberg, A. 2007. "The Phenomenology of Preschool Children's Spirituality." PhD diss., Queensland University of Technology, Brisbane, Australia.

Goleman, D. 1995. *Emotional Intelligence: Why It Can Matter More Than IQ.* New York: Bantam.

Goltsman, S. 2011. "Outdoor Play Settings: An Inclusive Approach." In *Universal Design Handbook,* 2nd ed., eds. W.F.E. Preiser & K.H. Smith, 22.1–22.10. New York: McGraw Hill.

Gopnik, A., A.N. Meltzoff, & P.K. Kuhl. 2001. *The Scientist in the Crib: What Early Learning Tells Us About the Mind.* New York: HarperCollins Books.

Grandjean, P., & P.J. Landrigan. 2014 "Neurobehavioural Effects of Developmental Toxicity." *The Lancet Neurology* 13 (3): 330–38.

Harris, K.I. 2007. "Re-Conceptualizing Spirituality in the Light of Educating Young Children." *International Journal of Children's Spirituality* 12 (3): 263–75.

Hart, R. 1978. *Children's Experience of Place: A Developmental Approach.* New York: Irvington.

Hawken, P. 2007. *Blessed Unrest: How the Largest Social Movement in History is Restoring Grace, Justice, and Beauty to the World.* New York: Penguin.

Heerwagen, J.H., & G.H. Orians. 2002. "The Ecological World of Children." In *Children and Nature: Psychological, Sociocultural, and Evolutionary Investigations,* eds. P.H. Kahn Jr. & S.R. Kellert, 29–64. Cambridge, MA: MIT Press.

Honig, A.S. 2002. *Secure Relationships: Infant/Toddler Attachment in Early Care Settings.* Washington, DC: NAEYC.

Hotchkiss, A.K., C.V. Rider, C.R. Blystone, V.S. Wilson, P.C. Hartig, G.T. Ankley, P.M. Foster, C.L. Gray, & L.E. Gray. 2008. "Fifteen Years After "Wingspread"—Environmental Endocrine Disrupters and Human and Wildlife Health: Where We are Today and Where We Need to Go." *Toxicological Sciences* 105 (2): 235–59. www.ncbi.nlm.nih.gov/pmc/articles/PMC2721670/.

Jarrett, O.S. 2013. "A Research-Based Case for Recess." US Play Coalition White Paper. http://usplaycoalition.clemson.edu/resources/articles/13.11.5_Recess_final_online.pdf.

KaBOOM! 2009. *Play Matters: A Study of Best Practices to Inform Local Policy and Process in Support of Children's Play.* Washington DC: KaBOOM! www.kaboom.org/docs/documents/pdf/playmatters/Play_Matters_Extended_Case_Studies.pdf.

Kagan, J. 2004. "The Uniquely Human in Human Nature." *Daedalus* 133 (4): 77–88.

Katz, L.G., & S.J. Katz. 2009. *Intellectual Emergencies: Some Reflections on Mothering and Teaching.* Louisville, NC: Kaplan Press.

Kable, J. 2010. "Theory of Loose Parts." *Let the Children Play* (blog). www.letthechildren play.net/2010/01/how-children-use-outdoor-play-spaces.html.

Keeler, R. 2008. *Natural Playscapes: Creating Outdoor Play Environments for the Soul.* Redmond, WA: Exchange Press.

Kellert, S.R. 2005. *Building for Life: Designing and Understanding the Human–Nature Connection.* Washington, DC: Island Press.

Kellert, S.R. 2012. *Birthright: People and Nature in the Modern World.* New Haven, CT: Yale University Press.

Kellert, S.R., & E.O. Wilson, eds. 1993. *The Biophilia Hypothesis.* Washington, DC: Island Press.

Kenny, E.K. 2013. *Forest Kindergartens: The Cedarsong Way.* Vashon, WA: Cedarsong Nature School.

Kim, E., & J. Lim. 2007. "Eco-Early Childhood Education: A New Paradigm of Early Childhood Education in South Korea." *Young Children* 62 (6): 42–45.

Kirchen, D.J. 2011. "Making and Taking Virtual Field Trips in Pre-K and the Primary Grades." *Young Children* 66 (6): 22–26.

Kirmani, M.H., & S. Kirmani. 2009. "Recognition of Seven Spiritual Identities and Its Implications for Children." *International Journal of Children's Spirituality* 14 (4): 369–83

Krathwohl, D.R., B.S. Bloom, & B.B. Masia. 1964. *Taxonomy of Educational Objectives, The Classification of Educational Goals. Handbook II: Affective Domain.* New York: David McKay.

Kuo, F.E. (Ming). 2010. *Parks and Other Green Environments: Essential Components of a Healthy Human Habitat. Executive Summary.* Ashburn, VA: National Recreation and Park Association. www.nrpa.org/uploadedFiles/nrpa.org/Publications_and_Research/Research/Papers/MingKuo-Summary.PDF.

Lally, J.R., P.L. Mangione, & D. Greenwald, eds. 2006. *Concepts for Care: 20 Essays on Infant/Toddler Development and Learning.* San Francisco, CA: WestEd.

Landrigan, P.J., L.Lambertini, & L.S. Birnbaum. 2012. "A Research Strategy to Discover the Environmental Causes of Autism and Neurodevelopmental Disabilities." *Environmental Health Perspectives* (120) 7: a258–a260. www.panna.org/sites/default/files/Autism_editorial_final_0.pdf.

Lanza, M. 2012. *Playborhood: Turn Your Neighborhood Into a Place for Play.* Menlo Park, CA: Free Play Press.

Larimore, R.A. 2011. *Establishing a Nature-Based Preschool.* Fort Collins, CO: InterpPress.

Leopold, A. 1949. *A Sand County Almanac.* New York: Ballantine.

Louv, R. 2005. *Last Child in the Woods: Saving Our Children from Nature-Deficit Disorder.* Chapel Hill, NC: Algonquin Books.

Louv, R. 2008. *Last Child in the Woods: Saving Our Children From Nature-Deficit Disorder.* Updated and expanded ed. Chapel Hill, NC: Algonquin Books.

Louv, R. 2012. *The Nature Principle: Reconnecting With Life in a Virtual Age.* Chapel Hill, NC: Algonquin Books.

Lucas, Bill. 1994. "Learning Through Landscapes." Speech at the International Symposium of the Montessori Foundation and the American Horticultural Society, Arlington, VA.

Mankiw, S. 2011. "Sun Safety." *Teaching Young Children* 4 (5): 23.

Maryland State Department of Education. 2012. *A Practical Guide to Planning, Constructing, and Using School Courtyards.* Baltimore, MD: Maryland State Department of Education. www.marylandpublicschools.org/NR/rdonlyres/FCB60C1D-6CC2-4270-BDAA-153D67247324/32899/PlanningConstructingUsingSchoolCourtyards_062012_.pdf.

McLennan, J.F. 2011. "Our Children's Cities: The Logic and Beauty of a Child-Centered Civilization." *Trim Tab* 10: 18–35. http://issuu.com/ecotone/docs/trimtabv10_summer2011/1.

McNamara, C. 2007. "Basic Definition of Organizations." http://managementhelp.org/organizations/definition.htm.

Meade, R. 2010. "State of Play: How Tot Lots Became Places to Build Children's Brains," *New Yorker*, July 5, 2010, 32–37.

Montessori, M. 1912 [1964]. *The Montessori Method.* New York: Schocken.

Montessori, M. 1963. *The Secret of Childhood* (B.B. Carter, trans.). Bombay, India: Orient Longmans.

Montessori, M. 1967. *The Absorbent Mind* (C.A. Claremont, trans.). New York: Dell.

Moore, R.C. 1986. *Childhood's Domain: Play and Place in Child Development.* London: Croon Helm.

Moore, R.C. 1992. *Play for All Guidelines: Planning, Design and Management of Outdoor Play Settings for All Children.* 2nd ed. Berkeley, CA: MIG Communications.

Moore, R.C. 1993. *Plants for Play: A Plant Selection Guide for Children's Outdoor Environments.* Berkeley, CA: MIG Communications.

Moore, R.C., & N.G. Cosco. 2007a. "Greening Montessori Schools Grounds by Design." *The NAMTA Journal* 32 (1): 129–51. www.naturalearning.org/sites/default/files/GreeningMontessoriDesign.pdf.

Moore, R.C., & N.G. Cosco. 2007b. "What Makes a Park Inclusive and Universally Designed? A Multi-Method Approach." In *Open Space: People Space*, eds. C.W. Thompson & P. Travlou, 85–110. New York: Taylor & Francis. www.naturalearning.org/sites/default/files/Moore_RandCosco_N_WhatMakesAParkInclusive.pdf.

Moore, R.C., & C.C. Marcus. 2008. "Healthy Planet, Healthy Children: Designing Nature Into the Daily Spaces of Childhood." In *Biophilic Design: The Theory, Science, and Practice of Bringing Buildings to Life,* eds. S.R. Kellert, J.H. Heerwagen, & M.L. Mador, 153–203. Hoboken, NJ: Wiley. www.naturalearning.org/sites/default/files/MooreCooperMarcus_Healthy.pdf.

Mustakova-Possardt, E. 2004. "Education for Critical Moral Consciousness." *Journal of Moral Education* 33 (3): 245–69.

Mustard, J.F. 2006. "Early Child Development and Experience-Based Brain Development: The Scientific Underpinnings of the Importance of Early Child Development in a Globalized World." Paper presented at The World Bank International Symposium on Early Childhood Development—A Priority for Sustained Economic Growth and Equity, Washington, DC, September 27–29, 2005. www.brookings.edu/views/papers/200602mustard.pdf.

NAEYC. 2008. *Standard 10: Leadership and Management—A Guide to the NAEYC Early Childhood Program Standard and Related Accreditation Criteria.* Washington, DC: NAEYC.

NAEYC. 2011. "What Are Forest Schools?" In *Spotlight on Young Children and Nature,* ed. A. Shillady, 52. Washington DC: NAEYC.

National Association for Sport and Physical Education (NASPE). 2006. "Recess for Elementary School Students." Position statement. www.aahperd.org/naspe/standards/upload/recess-for-elementary-school-students-2006.pdf.

National Center for Safe Routes to School. 2011. "How Children Get to School: School Travel Patterns From 1969 to 2009." http://saferoutesinfo.org/sites/default/files/resources/NHTS_school_travel_report_2011_0.pdf.

National Oceanic and Atmospheric Administration (NOAA). 2009. "Dead Zones: Hypoxia in the Gulf of Mexico." Silver Spring, MD: US Department of Commerce, NOAA. www.noaa.gov/factsheets/new%20version/dead_zones.pdf.

National Park Service. 2009. "Pathways to Healthy Living: More About Health—Current NPS Initiatives." www.nps.gov/ncrc/portals/health/more_abt_health.htm.

National Park Service. 2011. *Healthy Parks Healthy People US: Strategic Action Plan.* Washington, DC: National Park Service. www.nps.gov/public_health/hp/hphp/press/1012-955-WASO.pdf.

National Policy and Legal Analysis Network to Prevent Childhood Obesity, Public Health Law and Policy, & KaBOOM! 2012. *Playing Smart: Maximizing the Potential of School and Community Property Through Joint Use Agreements.* Washington, DC: Public Health Law and Policy. www.changelabsolutions.org/sites/phlpnet.org/files/Playing_Smart-National_Joint_Use_Toolkit_FINAL_20120309.pdf.

National Recreation and Park Association. 2011. *Parks and Recreation in Underserved Areas: A Public Health Perspective.* Ashburn, VA: National Recreation and Park Association. Accessed November 11. www.nrpa.org/uploadedFiles/nrpa.org/Publications_and_Research/Research/Papers/Parks-Rec-Underserved-Areas.pdf.

National Research Council. 1993. *Pesticides in the Diets of Infants and Children.* Washington, DC: The National Academies Press.

National Scientific Council on the Developing Child. 2007. *The Science of Early Childhood Development: Closing the Gap Between What We Know and What We Do.* Cambridge, MA: Harvard University, Center on the Developing Child. http://developingchild.harvard.edu/resources/reports_and_working_papers/science_of_early_childhood_development/.

Natural Learning Initiative and Center for Universal Design. 2005. "Post Occupancy Evaluation (POE) of Kids Together Park." Research Project Summary Report. www.ncsu.edu/ncsu/design/cud/about_us/docs/KTP-POE_Report_March-05.pdf.

Nature Explore. 2007. *Learning With Nature Idea Book: Creating Nurturing Outdoor Spaces for Children.* Lincoln, NE: Arbor Day Foundation and Dimensions Educational Research Foundation.

Nature Explore. 2011. *Growing With Nature: Supporting Whole-Child Learning in Outdoor Classrooms.* Lincoln, NE: Arbor Day Foundation and Dimensions Educational Research Foundation.

Nature Explore. 2012. *Keeping It Growing: Sustaining Your Outdoor Classroom.* Lincoln, NE: Arbor Day Foundation and Dimensions Educational Research Foundation.

Nelson, E.M. 2012. *Cultivating Outdoor Classrooms: Designing and Implementing Child-Centered Learning Environments.* St. Paul, MN: Redleaf Press.

New Canaan Nature Center Preschool. 2012. "Preschool Curriculum." www.newcanaannature.org/programs/preschool.

Nicol, J., & J.T. Taplin. 2012. *Understanding the Steiner Waldorf Approach.* Early Years Education in Practice Series, eds. P. Brunton & L. Thornton. New York: Routledge.

North American Association for Environmental Education. 2010. *Early Childhood Environmental Education Programs: Guidelines for Excellence.* Washington, DC: North American Association for Environmental Education. http://resources.spaces3.com/91ecfc06-2076-4e26-880d-2332e87b5caf.pdf.

O'Brien, L., & R. Murray. 2006. *A Marvellous Opportunity for Children to Learn: A Participatory Evaluation of Forest School in England and Wales.* Surrey: Forestry Commission England; Forest Research. www.forestry.gov.uk/pdf/fr0112forestschoolsreportpdf/$FILE/fr0112forestschoolsreport.pdf.

Office of Dietary Supplements. 2011. "Vitamin D: Fact Sheet for Health Professionals." www.ods.od.nih.gov/factsheets/VitaminD-HealthProfessional/.

Office of Environmental Justice. 2011. *Plan EJ 2014.* Washington, DC: US Environmental Protection Agency, Office of Environmental Justice. http://www.epa.gov/compliance/ej/resources/policy/plan-ej-2014/plan-ej-2011-09.pdf.

Olds, A.R. 2001. *Child Care Design Guide.* New York: McGraw-Hill.

Organisation for Economic Co-operation and Development (OECD). 2013. "Crisis Squeezes Income and Puts Pressure on Inequality and Poverty: New Results From the OECD Income Distribution Database." www.oecd.org/els/soc/OECD2013-Inequality-and-Poverty-8p.pdf.

Ostroff, E. 2011. "Universal Design: An Evolving Paradigm." In *Universal Design Handbook,* 2nd ed., eds. W.F.E. Preiser & K.H. Smith, 1.3–1.11. New York: McGraw Hill.

Pelo, A. 2009. "A Pedagogy for Ecology." *Rethinking Schools* 23 (4): 30–35.

Pelo, A. 2013. *The Goodness of Rain: Developing an Ecological Identity in Young Children.* Redmond, WA: Exchange Press.

Pesticide Action Network of North America (PANNA). 2012. *Pesticides and Honey Bees: State of the Science.* San Francisco, CA: PANNA. www.panna.org/issues/publication/pesticides-and-honey-bees-state-science.

Phenice, L.A., & R.J. Griffore. 2003. "Young Children and the Natural World." *Contemporary Issues in Early Childhood* 4 (2): 167–71.

Platt, L. 2012. "'Parks Are Dangerous and the Sidewalk Is Closer': Children's Use of Neighborhood Space in Milwaukee, Wisconsin." *Children, Youth and Environments* 22 (2): 194–213. www.colorado.edu/journals/cye/22_2/22_2_09_Milwaukee.pdf.

Project Learning Tree. 2010. *Environmental Experiences for Early Childhood.* Washington DC: American Forest Foundation.

Project WILD. 2012. *Growing Up WILD: Exploring Nature With Young Children Ages 3–7.* 2nd ed. Houston, TX: Council for Environmental Education.

Pyle, R.M. 1993. *The Thunder Tree: Lessons From an Urban Wildland.* New York: The Lyons Press.

Raikes, H.H., & C.P. Edwards. 2009. *Extending the Dance in Infant & Toddler Caregiving: Enhancing Attachment and Relationships.* Baltimore, MD: Brookes; Washington, DC: NAEYC.

Rinaldi, C. 2006. *In Dialogue With Reggio Emilia: Listening, Researching, and Learning.* London: Routledge.

Rivkin, M. 1997. "The Schoolyard Habitat Movement: What It Is and Why Children Need It." *Early Childhood Education Journal* 25 (1): 61–66. Also at National Wildlife Federation: www.nwf.org/How-to-Help/Garden-for-Wildlife/Schoolyard-Habitats/Benefits/The-Schoolyard-Habitat-Movement.aspx.

Rivkin, M. 2011. "Schools Going Green: Benefits for Children and Nature." In *Spotlight on Young Children and Nature*, ed. A. Shillady, 38–43. Washington, DC: NAEYC.

Roberts, A.L., K. Lyall, J.E. Hart, F. Laden, A.C. Just, J.F. Bobb, K.C. Koenen, A. Ascherio, & M.G. Weisskopf. 2013. "Perinatal Air Pollutant Exposures and Autism Spectrum Disorder in the Children of Nurses' Health Study II participants." *Environmental Health Perspectives* 121: 978–984. http://ehp.niehs.nih.gov/wp-content/uploads/121/8/ehp.1206187.pdf.

Roehlkepartain, E.C., P.E. King, L. Wagener, & P.L. Benson, eds. 2006. *The Handbook of Spiritual Development in Childhood and Adolescence.* Thousand Oaks, CA: Sage.

Rosen, C. J. 2010. "Lead in the Home Garden and the Urban Soil Environment." University of Minnesota Extension Service. http:// www.extension.umn.edu/distribution/horticulture/DG2543.html.

Rosenow, N. 2011. "Learning to Love the Earth . . . and Each Other." In *Spotlight on Young Children and Nature*, ed. A. Shillady, 4–7. Washington, DC: NAEYC.

Ross, B., & S. Amter. 2010. *The Polluters: The Making of Our Chemically Altered Environment.* New York: Oxford University Press.

Safe Routes to School National Partnership. 2012. "2011–2012 Summary Annual Report." Accessed November 2. www.saferoutesinfo.org/data-central/national-progress/federal-reports/2011-2012-annual-report.

Schafer, K. 2012. "A Big Step Towards Stronger Chemical Policy." *Ground Truth* (blog). www.panna.org/blog/big-step-towards-stronger-chemical-policy.

Schäffer, S.D., & T. Kistemann. 2012. "German Forest Kindergartens: Healthy Childcare Under the Leafy Canopy." *Children, Youth and Environments* 22 (1): 270–79.

Schein, D.L. 2012. "Early Childhood Educators' Perceptions of Spiritual Development in Young Children: A Social Constructivist Grounded Theory Study." PhD diss., Walden University. ProQuest Dissertations and Theses, DAI/A 74-05(E), publication number 3547107.

Schoolyard Habitat Partnership. 2010. *Toolkit for Schoolyard Habitat Program Development.* US Fish & Wildlife, Chesapeake Bay, Annapolis, MD. www.fws.gov/chesapeakebay/SCHOOL/PDF/SchoolyardProgramToolkit.pdf.

Schwab, J. 1969. "The Practical: A Language for Curriculum." *School Review* 78 (1): 1–23.

Science and Environmental Health Network. 2013. "Wingspread Conference on the Precautionary Principle, January 26, 1998." www.sehn.org/wing.html.

Shabecoff, P., & A. Shabecoff. 2008. *Poisoned Profits: The Toxic Assault on Our Children.* New York: Random House.

Shonkoff, J. P., & D.A. Phillips, eds. 2000. *From Neurons to Neighborhoods: The Science of Early Childhood Development.* Report of the National Research Council. Washington, DC: The National Academies Press.

Siegel, D.J., & M. Hartzell. 2003. *Parenting From the Inside Out: How a Deeper Self-Understanding Can Help You Raise Children Who Thrive.* New York: Tarcher/Penguin.

Skin Cancer Foundation. 2012. "Choosing Sunglasses for Your Kids." Accessed July 8. www.skincancer.org/prevention/sun-protection/children/choosing-sunglasses-for-your-kids.

Skin Cancer Foundation. 2014. "Five Ways to Treat a Sunburn." Accessed March 1. www.skincancer.org/prevention/sunburn/five-ways-to-treat-a-sunburn.

Smart Growth America & National Complete Streets Coalition. 2012. *Complete Streets Policy Analysis 2011.* Washington, DC: Smart Growth America. www.smartgrowthamerica.org/documents/cs/resources/cs-policyanalysis.pdf.

Smart Growth America & National Complete Streets Coalition. 2014. *The Best Complete Streets Policies of 2013.* Washington, DC: Smart Growth America. www.smartgrowthamerica.org/documents/best-complete-streets-policies-of-2013.pdf.

Sobel, D. 2004. *Place-Based Education, Connecting Classrooms and Communities.* Great Barrington, MA: The Orion Society.

Sobel, D. 2008. *Childhood and Nature: Design Principles for Educators.* Portland, ME: Stenhouse.

Sobel, D. 2012. "Look, Don't Touch: The Problem With Environmental Education." *Orion* 31 (4): 64–71.

Stanford Center on Poverty and Inequality. 2012. "One of Twenty Facts About U.S. Inequality That Everyone Should Know: Child Poverty." Accessed July 23. www.stanford.edu/group/scspi/cgi-bin/facts.php.

Stanford Center on Poverty and Inequality. 2014. "The Poverty and Inequality Report." Executive summary. www.stanford.edu/group/scspi/sotu/SOTU_2014_executive-summary.pdf.

State of California. 2002. "An Act to Amend Section 35183.5 of the Education Code, Relating to Pupil Health." Bill Number SB 1632. www.leginfo.ca.gov/pub/01-02/bill/sen/sb_1601-1650/sb_1632_bill_20020826_chaptered.html.

State of Maryland. 2009. "Maryland Children's Outdoor Bill of Rights." www.governor.maryland.gov/documents/OutdoorBillOfRights.pdf.

Steingraber, S. 2010. *Living Downstream: An Ecologist's Personal Investigation of Cancer and the Environment.* 2nd ed. Cambridge, MA: Da Capo Press.

Steingraber, S. 2011. *Raising Elijah: Protecting Our Children in an Age of Environmental Crisis.* Boston, MA: Da Capo Press.

Stone, C., D. Trisi, A. Sherman, & W. Chen. 2013. *A Guide to Statistics on Historical Trends in Income Inequality.* Washington, DC: Center on Budget and Policy Priorities. www.cbpp.org/files/11-28-11pov.pdf.

Sucher, D. 2003. *City Comforts: How to Build an Urban Village.* Rev. ed. Seattle, WA: City Comforts.

Sullivan, W.C., F.E. Kuo, & S.F. DePooter. 2004. "The Fruit of Urban Nature: Vital Neighborhood Spaces." *Environment and Behavior* 36 (5): 678–700.

Surr, John. 2011. "Links Between Early Attachment Experiences and Manifestations of Spirituality." *International Journal of Children's Spirituality* 16 (2): 129–41.

Sutton, S.E., & S.P. Kemp. 2011. *The Paradox of Urban Space: Inequality and Transformation in Marginalized Communities.* New York: Palgrave Macmillan.

Synthetic Turf Council. 2008. "U.S. CPSC Validates Safety of Lead Chromate in Synthetic Turf and STC Announces Voluntary Reduction." www.syntheticturfcouncil.org/news/123932/U.S.-CPSC-Validates-Safety-of-Lead-Chromate-in-Synthetic-Turf-and-STC-Announces-Voluntary-Reduction.htm.

Tallamy, D.W. 2009. *Bringing Nature Home: How You Can Sustain Wildlife With Native Plants.* Updated and Expanded. Portland, OR: Timber Press.

Tamez, M. 2012. "On Being 'Indian,' Unsilent, and Contaminated Along the US-Mexico Border." In *Companions in Wonder—Children and Adults Exploring Nature Together,* eds. S. Kellert & J. Dunlap, 251–57. Cambridge, MA: MIT Press.

Tandon, P.S., C. Zhou, & D.A. Christakis. 2012. "Frequency of Parent-Supervised Outdoor Play of US Preschool-Aged Children." *Archives of Pediatrics and Adolescent Medicine* 166 (8): 707–12.

Taylor, A.F., & F.E. Kuo. 2008. "Children With Attention Deficits Concentrate Better After Walk in the Park." *Journal of Attention Disorders* 12: 402–9.

Titman, W. 1994. *Special Places, Special People: The Hidden Curriculum of School Grounds.* Toronto: Green Brick Road.

Trust for Public Land. 2012. "Parks for People." www.tpl.org/our-work/parks-for-people.

Tuan, Y.F. 1993. *Passing Strange and Wonderful: Aesthetics, Nature, and Culture.* Washington, DC: Island Press; Covelo, CA: Shearwater.

UN General Assembly. 1989. *Convention on the Rights of the Child.* United Nations, Treaty Series, vol. 1577. www.ohchr.org/Documents/ProfessionalInterest/crc.pdf.

UNICEF. 2012. "What Is a Child Friendly City?" Accessed July 23. www.childfriendlycities.org/overview/what-is-a-child-friendly-city/.

United Nations, Department of Economic and Social Affairs, Population Division. 2012. *World Urbanization Prospects, the 2011 Revision: Highlights.* New York: United Nations. http://esa.un.org/unpd/wup/Documentation/highlights.htm.

US Bureau of Labor Statistics. 2013. "Employment Characteristics of Families—2012." www.bls.gov/news.release/pdf/famee.pdf.

US Consumer Product Safety Commission (CPSC). 2010. *Public Playground Safety Handbook.* Bethesda, MD: US CPSC. www.cpsc.gov/PageFiles/107329/325.pdf.

US Department of Education. 2012. "US Department of Education Green Ribbon Schools—Eligibility." www2.ed.gov/programs/green-ribbon-schools/eligibility.html.

US Environmental Protection Agency (EPA). 2008. "Wetlands and Wonder: Reconnecting Children With Nearby Nature." DVD. http://water.epa.gov/type/wetlands/outreach/wetlandsvideo_index.cfm.

US Environmental Protection Agency (EPA). 2010. "Revisions to Lead Ambient Air Monitoring Requirements." *Federal Register* 75 (247): 81126-81139. www.gpo.gov/fdsys/pkg/FR-2010-12-27/pdf/2010-32153.pdf.

US Environmental Protection Agency (EPA). 2011. "The US Environmental Protection Agency's Strategic Plan for Evaluating the Toxicity of Chemicals." www.epa.gov/spc/toxicitytesting.

van Leeuwen, M., & J. Moeskops. 2008. *The Nature Corner: Celebrating the Year's Cycle With Seasonal Tableaux*. 2nd ed. Edinburgh: Floris Books.

Vandell, D.L. 2004. "Early Child Care: The Known and the Unknown." *Merrill-Palmer Quarterly* 50 (3): 387–414.

Vandenberg, L., T. Colborn, T.B. Hayes, J.J. Heindel, D.R. Jacobs, Jr., D.-H. Lee, T. Shioda, A.M. Soto, F.S. vom Saal, W.V. Welshons, R.T. Zoeller, & J.P. Myers. 2012. "Hormones and Endocrine-Disrupting Chemicals: Low-Dose Effects and Nonmonotonic Dose Responses." *Endocrine Review* 33 (3): 378–455. http://edrv.endojournals.org/content/early/2012/03/14/er.2011-1050.full.pdf+html.

Vygotsky, L.S. 1962. *Thought and Language* (E. Hanfmann & G. Vakar, eds. & trans.). Cambridge, MA: MIT Press.

Warden, C. 2012. *Nature Kindergartens and Forest Schools: An Exploration of Naturalistic Learning Within Nature Kindergartens and Forest Schools.* 2nd ed. Auchterarder, Scotland, UK: Mindstretchers.

Watson, J. 2012. "Starting Well: Benchmarking Early Education Across the World." *The Economist* Intelligence Unit. Summary at www.managementthinking.eiu.com/starting-well.html.

Weinberg, D.H. 2011. *US Neighborhood Income Inequality in the 2005–2009 Period.* American Community Survey Reports. US Department of Commerce, US Census Bureau. www.census.gov/prod/2011pubs/acs-16.pdf.

White, J. 2012. *Making a Mud Kitchen.* Sheffield, UK: Muddyfaces. www.muddyfaces.co.uk/mud_kitchens.php.

White, J. 2014. *Playing and Learning Outdoors: Making Provision for High-Quality Experiences in the Outdoor Environment with Children 3–7.* 2nd ed. London: Routledge.

Williams-Siegfredsen, J. 2012. *Understanding the Danish Forest School Approach.* Early Years Education in Practice Series, eds. P. Brunton & L. Thornton. New York: Routledge.

Wilson, E.O. 1984. *Biophilia: The Human Bond With Other Species.* Cambridge, MA: Harvard University Press.

Wilson, E.O. 2008. "The Nature of Human Nature." In *Biophilic Design: The Theory, Science, and Practice of Bringing Buildings to Life*, eds. S.R. Kellert, J.H. Heerwagen, & M.L. Mador, 21–25. Hoboken, NJ: John Wiley & Sons.

Wilson, R.A. 2012a. "Developing the Whole Child: Celebrating the Spirit of Each Child." *Earlychildhood NEWS.* Accessed September 13. www.earlychildhoodnews.com/earlychildhood/article_view.aspx?ArticleID=545.

Wilson, R.A. 2012b. *Nature and Young Children: Encouraging Creative Play and Learning in Natural Environments.* 2nd ed. New York: Routledge.

Zhu, P., & Y. Zhang. 2008. "Demand for Urban Forests in United States Cities." *Landscape and Urban Planning* 84 (3–4): 293–300.

Organizations and Other Groups Referenced in *The Great Outdoors*

American Academy of Pediatrics
www.aap.org

American Community Gardening Association
www.communitygarden.org

Arbor Day Foundation
www.arborday.org

Baltimore's Parks and People Foundation
http://parksandpeople.org/

Bay Watershed Education and Training
(B-WET) Program
www.oesd.noaa.gov/grants/bwet.html#page=about

The Biosophical Institute
http://biosophical.org

BlueCross BlueShield Association
www.bcbs.com

The Boston Schoolyard Initiative
www.schoolyards.org

Boston Schoolyards Funders Collaborative
www.schoolyards.org/about.collab.html

The Campaign for Safe Cosmetics
www.safecosmetics.org

The Carolina Thread Trail
www.carolinathreadtrail.org

Cedarsong Nature School
www.cedarsongnatureschool.org

Center for Environmental Health
www.ceh.org

Centers for Disease Control and Prevention
www.cdc.gov

Child Friendly Cities Initiative
www.childfriendlycities.org

Child Rights Campaign
www.childrightscampaign.org

Children and Nature Network
www.childrenandnature.org

Children's Defense Fund
www.childrensdefense.org

The Children's Environmental Health Network
www.cehn.org

Chippewa Nature Center
http://chippewanaturecenter.org

The Cooperative Extension System of the
US Department of Agriculture
www.csrees.usda.gov/Extension

Dimensions Educational Research Foundation
www.dimensionsfoundation.org

Dodge Nature Center
www.dodgenaturecenter.org

Economist Intelligence Unit
www.eiu.com/home.aspx

Eco-Schools
www.nwf.org/Eco-Schools-USA.aspx

Environmental Protection Agency
www.epa.gov

Environmental Protection Agency's UV Index
www2.epa.gov/sunwise/uv-index

The Environmental Working Group
www.ewg.org

Green Schools National Network
http://greenschoolsnationalnetwork.org

GreenHearts
www.greenheartsinc.org

The Growing Up In Cities Project
www.unesco.org/most/guic/guicmain.htm

International School Grounds Alliance
www.greenschoolyards.org

Irvine Nature Center
www.explorenature.org

KaBOOM!
http://kaboom.org

Kalamazoo Nature Center
www.naturecenter.org

Let the Children Play
www.letthechildrenplay.net

The Maryland Association for Environmental and
Outdoor Education
www.maeoe.org

Maryland Department of Natural Resources
www.dnr.state.md.us/

The Massachusetts Audubon Society
www.massaudubon.org

National Association for Sport and
Physical Education
www.aahperd.org/naspe/

National Complete Streets Coalition
www.smartgrowthamerica.org/complete-streets

National Lead Information Center
www2.epa.gov/lead/forms/lead-hotline-national-lead-information-center

National Park Service
www.nps.gov

The National Park Service's Program, Rivers,
Trails, and Conservation Assistance
www.nps.gov/rtca

The National Pesticide Information Center
www.npic.orst.edu

National Toxicology Program
http://ntp.niehs.nih.gov/

The National Trails Training Partnership
www.Americantrails.org/resources

National Wildlife Federation
www.nwf.org

Natural Learning Initiative
www.naturalearning.org

The Natural Start Alliance
http://naturalstart.org

The Nature Conservancy
www.nature.org

Nature Explore
www.natureexplore.org

Nature Rocks
www.naturerocks.org

North American Association for Environmental
Education
www.naaee.net

The Partnership for a Healthier America
http://ahealthieramerica.org/

The Pesticide Action Network North America
www.panna.org

Pew Charitable Trusts
www.pewtrusts.org

The PlayPod Program
www.playpods.co.uk

The Playworks Program
www.playworks.org

Project Learning Tree
www.plt.org

Project WILD
www.projectwild.org

The Robert Wood Johnson Foundation
www.rwjf.org

Science and Environmental Health Network
http://sehn.org

Skin Cancer Foundation
www.skincancer.org

Smart Growth America
www.smartgrowthamerica.org

Stanford Center on Poverty and Inequality
www.stanford.edu/group/scspi/

Sun Safety for Kids
www.sunsafetyforkids.org

Transportation for America
http://t4america.org

The Trust for Public Land
www.tpl.org

Tule Elk Park
www.tuleelkpark.org

UNICEF
www.unicef.org

The United Nations Educational, Scientific and Cultural Organization
http://en.unesco.org

United Nations
www.un.org/en/

The US Consumer Product Safety Commission
www.cpsc.gov

US Department of Agriculture
www.usda.gov

US Department of Education
www.ed.gov

US Department of the Interior
www.doi.gov

US Department of Transportation
www.dot.gov

US Fish and Wildlife Service
www.fws.gov

About the Authors

Mary Rivkin, PhD, is an associate professor of education at the University of Maryland, Baltimore County. Her research focuses on children's outdoor play. In addition to numerous articles about outdoor play for young children and the first edition of *The Great Outdoors*, Mary wrote, with Jean D. Harlan, *Science Experiences for the Early Childhood Years*, which is currently in its tenth edition and has been translated into several languages. She was a member of the writing team for *Early Childhood Environmental Education Programs: Guidelines for Excellence*, which was published by the North American Association for Environmental Education. Mary also worked for the National Science Foundation and taught elementary school and nursery school.

One of Mary's concerns is that all children, especially children in developed countries, lack direct experience with nature, resulting in a weak connection to joy and learning that can happen in outdoor environments. Given recent research that confirms what many have known all along, that nature is good for us, Mary hopes to inspire educators to work harder to conserve natural environments for all children.

Mary lives in Maryland with her husband Steve.

Deborah Schein, PhD, teaches at Champlain College and consults for the Agency of Jewish Learning in Pittsburgh. Deborah is a trained and certified Montessori teacher, an Early Childhood National Board Certified Teacher, and a Reggio Emilia study group facilitator and consultant. She has taught preschool children, college students, teachers, JCCA camp directors, and families. She is the coauthor of *What's Jewish About Butterflies: 36 Dynamic, Engaging Lessons for the Early Childhood Classroom* and has recently published articles for the CCAR and NRJE on early childhood spiritual development.

Acknowledgments

From Mary Rivkin

At UMBC, I am thankful to my department chair, Eugene Shaffer, for his granting me course releases for two semesters to give me time to work on the book, and to my early childhood colleagues, Sue Small, Peg Costello, Pat Scully, and Audrey Jewett, for their support and encouragement. Our early childhood students, willing travelers on the outdoor excursions, have contributed their enthusiasm and for this book some of their writings. Thanks to Alexandra Alton, Christie Cioffi, and Hayley Knudsen for sharing their stories.

At NAEYC, I am grateful to Derry Koralek, Kathy Charner, and Liz Wegner for their patience, understanding, and clever solutions. The designers Malini Dominey and Edwin Malstrom are amazing transformers and I thank them.

For developing an aspect of the relationship of children and nature that is usually overlooked— spirituality—I am indebted to Deb Schein for her research and writing. She filled a gap in this book.

For generosity with photos, many thanks to Bob and Patti Bailie, the Pedestrian Bicycle Information Center (PBCI), Mary Hardcastle and Parks and People, Sheila Ridge Williams and the Dodge Irvine Nature Preschool, and Mark Brennan.

For ongoing inspiration, I am grateful to Louise Chawla, Robin Moore, Richard Louv, Polly Greenberg, Sue Humphries, Mimi Brodsky Chenfeld, Nancy Wagner, Patti Bailie, Ann Pelo, Erin Kenny, and Olga Jarrett.

For practical experience in naturalizing a play space, thanks to Chris Peusch, Diane Mellot, Beth Grant, Jennifer Reynolds, Yolande Simms, and staff at Tawes Play and Learn Center, John Griffin, Britt Slattery, Amy Henry and Sandi Olek of MD Department of Natural Resources, Ron Rafter, Sam Cook, and Jordan Loran of the MD Department of General Services, Robin Moore for the conceptual design, and Karen Kelly Mullin, partner in numerous presentations about the Tawes play yard.

At home, I am deeply thankful for the patience and thoughtfulness of my husband Steve which held our home together with many good dinners, and much leaving me to work in my study. He also shared his well-honed editorial skills on many occasions. I am grateful to my siblings who share my love of nature based on our Pacific Northwest childhood—Edward Stimpson, Catharine Stimpson, Susan Trimingham, Jane Bremner, Caroline Macdonald, and John Stimpson. They have always understood what I was about. My children and their children motivate and validate this children and nature work. Thank you, Caroline Seckinger, Gustave Carlson, Belle Carlson, Keown Carlson, Robert Seckinger, Ina Clark, Maya Seckinger, Wiley Seckinger, Sarah Rivkin, Mark Brennan, Ceci Brennan, Toby Brennan, and Jesse Rivkin, whose curtailed outdoor play in the 1990s stirred me to writing the first edition of this book.

Age brings appreciation of those who have gone before, especially my mother who kept taking us on nature experiences, with guide books, and my father who made us memorize the names of the mountains around us and the constellations above us, and my grandfather who loved his terraced garden to his last months, and my grandmother who had a magical garden with a swing for each grandchild. Listening to my mother and grandmother talk about the flowers in that yard, and about which apples made the best applesauce, and which cows gave the richest milk, and so many other namings and describings of the world we were in, surely underlies my own intense interest in such causes as monarch butterflies and saving the local nature trail.

From Deborah Schein

First of all, thank you to Mary Rivkin for inviting me to share my research within her book; to Patti Bailie, who has been a partner and support throughout my research; to Amie Beckett, my guiding light; and to my husband Jeffrey, who continues to support me always in all that I do.